D0929236

BALLPARKS

BALLPARKS

A Panoramic History
5th Edition

MARC SANDALOW & JIM SUTTON
UPDATED BY LEW FREEDMAN

**CHARTWELL
BOOKS**

Brimming with creative inspiration, how-to projects, and useful information to enrich your everyday life, Quarto Knows is a favorite destination for those pursuing their interests and passions. Visit our site and dig deeper with our books into your area of interest: Quarto Creates, Quarto Cooks, Quarto Homes, Quarto Lives, Quarto Drives, Quarto Explores, Quarto Gifts, or Quarto Kids.

This edition published in 2017 by Chartwell Books
an imprint of The Quarto Group
142 West 36th Streeet, 4th Floor
New York, New York 10018
USA

© 2017 by Greene Media Ltd.

From an idea proposed by Frank Oppel

All rights reserved. No part of this publication may be reproduced, stored in a retrieval system or transmitted in any form or by any means, electronic, mechanical, photocopying, recording or otherwise, without the prior permission of Greene Media Ltd. All correspondence concerning the content of this volume should be addressed to Greene Media Ltd., c/o Chartwell Books.

ISBN: 978-0-7858-3575-2

Printed and bound in China

10 9 8 7 6 5 4 3 2 1

Design: Greene Media Ltd

Photographs
All images are credited with their captions. Photos came from Getty Images, Corbis, the Baseball Hall of Fame, Digitalballparks.com, Roger Miller, WikiCommons, and the *San Francisco Chronicle*: thanks to all those who helped.

Page 1: Looking toward Fenway Park's diamond in the 1950s. The "Green Monster" is on the right.
National Baseball Hall of Fame

Page 2: The F-16 Fighting Falcons of the Thunderbirds precision flying demonstration team perform a flyover during the national anthem at the MLB's All-Star Game July 15, 2014, Target Field, Minneapolis, MN.
U.S. Air Force photo/Master Sgt. Stan Parker

Above: A unique event took place at Fort Bragg, NC, on July 3, 2016: the first professional sporting contest at an active military base. It was played on a field that had been created for the event, the MLB and the union funding the $5 million construction costs of the 12,500-seater ballpark: stands, dugouts, bullpens, videoboards and all other requirements including, of course, an immaculate field measuring 331 feet down the foul lines, 387 to the power alleys and 405 to dead center. The Marlins won 5–2 with J.T. Realmuto having a three-hit night. The ballpark was temporary and will be converted into a "multipurpose recreational facility."
Streeter Lecka/Getty Images

CONTENTS

INTRODUCTION

Baseball is unique among American sports. Football, basketball, and hockey are played on identical fields, courts, and rinks. Only in baseball does the park define the game.

There is simply no feeling like walking into a ballpark on an early spring day and taking in the expanse of lush, green, meticulously groomed, and mostly uninhabited grass. There is a buzz, a smell, and an excitement to a baseball stadium that cannot be recreated on the evening news or the morning's sports pages, as dutifully as they try.

The Green Monster in Boston, the ivy in Chicago, the center field hill in Houston, the Bermuda Triangle in Miami, the convertible roof in Seattle, and the cove in San Francisco: these not only brand each park with a distinct appearance, they change the way the game is played.

There is little discussion of how many baskets Wilt Chamberlain would have shot, or how many goals Wayne Gretsky would have scored, had they spent their careers at the Boston Garden. Yet baseball fans can spend hours debating what Babe Ruth might have done as a Fenway slugger; how many home runs Willie Mays might have hit if not for the wind at Candlestick Park; or whether the Minnesota Twins would have won a world championship, let alone two, if not for the helpful horrors of their Metrodome. A game at Wrigley Field in Chicago is a very different experience than one at Dodger Stadium in Los Angeles, or Pro Player in Miami.

This book attempts to highlight those differences. It is not an authoritative account of baseball stadiums, or an encyclopedic telling of their history. Instead, it is a picture-filled look at what makes the current major league parks, and some of the famous old ones, so special.

To anyone trying to write about ballparks, it is quickly apparent that parks are in a perpetual state of change. Since Baltimore Memorial Stadium opened in 1954, well over forty new ballparks have been constructed, several of which have already been replaced and demolished. As this book was originally being researched, two ballparks changed their names, and two others shut their doors to make way for new ones. By next season, many of the parks described in this book will have undergone some renovations. To a baseball fan, the changes provide a fascinating glimpse at the game's evolution.

The quirkiness and intimacy of the turn-of-the century ballparks was largely the product of geography and finances, as team owners tried to cram stadiums into small urban lots, in places where fans would be plentiful. If the lot was misshaped, as at Washington's Griffith Stadium (where one home owner refused to budge from the stadium site), the crooked outfield wall was simply built around it. Fenway's Green Monster was erected because of the park's tight quarters, and to block residents on Lansdowne Street from getting a free look at the game. Such quirks are now carefully added to stadium designs, sometimes at great additional cost, to capture a sense of history and tradition.

Today, it is also an article of faith among baseball owners that stadiums should be intimate and small, built to boost home run totals to lure fans to the games. Yet in 1910, when Charlie Comiskey built a park on the south side of Chicago for his White Sox, he wanted a huge outfield, partly for the thrill of watching fielders make long sprints for balls, and for the excitement of watching runners try for extra base hits, rather than lope around the bases in a lazy home run trot.

A generation from now, the game will have evolved again. Perhaps the short fences that mark early 21st century parks will seem like dinosaurs. Just as the opening of steel-and-concrete Shibe Park in Philadelphia in 1909 and the opening of Oriole Park at Camden Yards in Baltimore in 1992 touched off revolutions in ballpark designs, it is easy to imagine some future innovation changing the look of baseball stadiums.

Some qualities seem certain to endure. The perfect diamond, the lush turf, the intimacy between the players and the fans, the geographic landmarks that let you know exactly where the game is being played. For 30 major league cities, there are few structures that better tell their story than their ballpark.

Fans are what it's all about. Will this new generation of Cubs' fans still be visiting Wrigley Field with their children? Victor Ireland, Jacob Peckerson, and Sinhue Mendoda show their loyalty to the Cubs before the game against the Florida Marlins, October 7, 2003.
Brian Bahr/Getty Images

The historian Jacques Barzun famously wrote: "Whoever wants to know the heart and mind of America, had better learn baseball." In a similar vein, whoever wants to know baseball had better learn ballparks. This book is a start.

Acknowledgments

Everyone has an opinion about ballparks. Thanks to Vernard Atkins, Zac Coile, Bob Congdon, Bonnie DeSimone, Ed Epstein, Carl Nolte, Marcie Sandalow, and Ellen Loerke for sharing their insightful views with us. Special thanks to Tom McClurg for his careful reading of the text and his constant reminder of what makes baseball great.

Many people helped in the hunt for photos. Special thanks to W.C. Burdick of the National Baseball Hall of Fame, Marc Seigerman at Getty Images, Gary Fong at the San Francisco Chronicle, Eric Pastore of Digital Ballparks. com, Rob Arra of Everlasting Images, Roger Miller of Baltimore's Roger Miller Studio Ltd., and to Sandra Forty.

Thank you, every one and all.

Jim Sutton, who died in late 2009, would have been directly involved in revising this new edition: an admirable researcher and publisher, he is sorely missed.

Exterior view of Camden Yards late in the afternoon of August 15, 2003, during the game between the Orioles and the Yankees. This retro design influenced a new generation of ballparks designed for baseball rather than ground-sharing with football. The new Marlins Park is the first to throw off this approach for a more modern 21st century design.
Jerry Driendl/Getty Images

THE AMERICAN LEAGUE

The roster of American League cities sounds like a refrain from a Chuck Berry song: Detroit, Chicago, Baltimore, Boston, and K.C. When it was founded in 1901, the American League was the junior circuit, coming to life a quarter of a century after the National League, and bringing professional baseball to America's thriving metropolises. Of the eight original American League cities, all still have a professional team.

Some American League teams have come and gone, such as the Boston Pilgrims, the Cleveland Naps, the Seattle Pilots, and the Washington Senators. Roughly fifty stadiums have been home to American League teams. Several of the old classics—Detroit's Tiger Stadium, Cleveland's Municipal Stadium, and Chicago's Comiskey Park—closed in the 1990s.

The American League's oldest stadium is Fenway Park, which opened the same week the *Titanic* sank in 1912. Exactly 80 years later, Baltimore's Camden Yards sparked a new wave of classic-style parks; structures which sought to imitate the intimacy of Fenway and other older parks. There are now new ballparks in Minnesota, New York (two of them) and Washington. With their lease of the O.co. Coliseum due to expire in 2015, the A's signed a 10-year lease (in 2014) with the Oakland-Alameda County Coliseum Authority; as part of the lease the latter has agreed to pay $1 million a year (with 5% annual increases) into a fund to maintain the stadium.

Fenway Park seen from inside the Boston Red Sox dugout during the game against the Yankees on July 25, 2003. Having celebrated its centenary in 2012, Fenway may have some of the problems of older stadiums—obstructed views—but it is still America's best-loved ballpark.
Jerry Driendl/Getty Images

AMERICAN LEAGUE EAST

The major change to the ballparks of the American League's Eastern Division is the loss of one of the most storied parks in baseball—Yankee Stadium—leaving Fenway Park as the only oldster. Fenway is where Babe Ruth began his career, and Yankee is where he reached power-hitting immortality. Ty Cobb, Walter Johnson, Hank Greenberg, Jimmy Foxx, Tris Speaker, each played on those very fields but only the Red Sox still play there. Fans can still sit in the same Boston bleachers where Ted Williams hit his longest shot, but no longer in Yankee Stadium where Lou Gehrig bid baseball adieu.

To the north, SkyDome—now the Rogers Centre—with its convertible roof, showed the sporting world how to handle the elements. Orioles Park at Camden Yard reminded fans of the game's intrinsic beauty, while Tropicana Field in Florida jammed in about as much entertainment as can fit inside a structure built for baseball.

The refurbishment of Fenway Park means that the venerable centenarian meets 21st century standards. The other parks of the American League Eastern Division largely look like they are here to stay, except for Tropicana. For years the Rays have discussed a new home, and during 2016 nine sites were identified as possibilities. A decision on which is unlikely to be swiftly forthcoming—and a finalization of the costs and who will pay them will be similarly thorny.

This photo: Oriole Park at Camden Yards during the game between the Orioles and the Yankees on August 14, 2003. The progenitor of the retro movement, Camden Yards influenced ballpark design for the next 20 years.
Jerry Driendl/Getty Images

BALTIMORE ORIOLES

ORIOLE PARK AT CAMDEN YARDS

Address:
333 West Camden Street
Baltimore, MD 21201
Capacity: 45,971
Opening day: April 6, 1992—Baltimore Orioles 2,
Cleveland Indians 0
Cost to construct: $110 million
Architect: HOK Sports
Dimensions (ft):
Left Field—333
Left Center—364
Center Field—410
Right Center—373
Right Field—318
Defining feature: B&O Warehouse in right field
Little-known ground rule: Fly ball hitting the grounds
crew shed roof in right field and bouncing back into play:
Home Run
World Series: None
All-Star Game: 1993
Memorable moments:
1993 July 13—Seattle's Ken Griffey Jr. becomes the first
    player to hit the B&O warehouse on a fly, during a
    home run contest preceding the All-Star game.
1995 September 6—Cal Ripken Jr. smacks a fourth-
    inning home run while playing in his 2131st
    consecutive game, surpassing Lou Gehrig as
    baseball's "Iron Man."
2012 September 13—By beating the Rays the Orioles
    reach their 81st victory of the season and go on
    to end their 14-year losing drought with a wild
    card berth against the Rangers. The Orioles win
    5–1 and play the Yankees for the ALDS.
2012 October 8—Victory for the Orioles over the
    Yankees, but they will come off worse overall 3–2.
2015 April 29—First ever game played to an empty
    stadium following local civil unrest.

The opening of Oriole Park at Camden Yards touched off a baseball revolution. After three decades of constructing cookie-cutter coliseums, Baltimore reintroduced the concept of a ballpark. Nestled beside train lines in the city's inner harbor, the yard was a throwback to the days of Babe Ruth, born just two blocks away. Its brick facade, asymmetrical outfield, panoramic view of downtown Baltimore, and the imposing B&O warehouse—which taunts left handed hitters—reminded Americans why baseball was long regarded as the national pastime.

The rest of baseball took notice. Within a decade, ballparks in Detroit, Seattle, Cleveland, Atlanta, Pittsburgh, San Francisco, Arlington, Milwaukee, Houston, and San Diego mimicked Baltimore's retro appeal.

Baseball history guided the architects, who were influenced by Ebbets Field (Brooklyn), Shibe Park (Philadelphia), Fenway Park (Boston), Crosley Field (Cincinnati), Forbes Field (Pittsburgh), Wrigley Field (Chicago), and the Polo Grounds (New York). The cozy dimensions, the steel trusses, the rustic clock on the center field scoreboard, all gave the park a classic feel.

But the park is new. It has luxury boxes (a major revenue source), microbrews, a family picnic area, and shiny bronze baseballs imbedded in Eutaw Street, which runs between the warehouse and the outfield bleachers. Just beyond the bleachers, fans can buy barbeque made by Oriole great Boog Powell, who can sometimes be found signing hot dog wrappers and ticket stubs.

The history is more than just appearance. Ruth's father owned a tavern about where center field now sits. The eight-story, red-bricked, turn of the century B&O warehouse, the park's defining feature, is more than 1,000 feet long, built in 1895 to handle long railroad freight cars, and is said to be the longest building on the East Coast. It sits 432 feet away from home plate and though Ken Griffey Jr. reached it during a home run competition before the 1993 All-Star Game, no one has yet done so during a game. The park's anchor in a revitalized downtown was a big reason that the legislature agreed to help pay for it with the sale of lottery tickets. When it was built, Maryland Governor William Donald Schaefer called the ballpark "the largest single economic development opportunity we have had in the last decade," and its success spurred other clubs to look beyond land-rich suburban areas for their stadium homes.

The move from Baltimore's old Memorial Stadium to Camden Yards "is like coming from the slums to a palace," Orioles' outfield David Segui said the week the park opened. "If we play half as good as this place looks we'll be pretty good this year." Unfortunately for O's fans, the park has fared better than the Orioles who are still looking to bring a World Series to Camden Yards.

It has long been acknowledged that when Oriole Park at Camden Yards opened in 1992, all of baseball sighed with envy—it seemed the perfect ballpark. After a quarter of a century Camden Yards has endured as a role model and trendsetter. The Major Leagues as a whole, not merely Orioles fans, owe a big thank-you to the park's designers who jolted the sport out of the construction doldrums and were pathfinders.

Since the opening of Camden Yards on April 6, 1992, 22 other teams have shown off new parks. The Orioles like to refer to Camden Yards as The Ballpark That Forever Changed Baseball—and given the ripple effect following the park's opening they have a right to do so.

Beginning in mid-January, as the 2017 anniversary season approached, the Orioles gradually unveiled a list to fans of the 25 most memorable moments in the history of the Park. The season opened on April 3 at home, not April 6, though, with a 3–2, 11-inning victory over Toronto. The Orioles had an off day on the actual April 6 anniversary.

However, the Orioles marked the 25th anniversary throughout the 2017 with special fan giveaways—including a replica model of Camden Yards.

Right: An April 2015 view of sunny Camden Yards as the Orioles prepare to take on the Red Sox.
Keith Allison via WikiCommons (CC BY-SA 2.0)

Night panorama of Oriole
Park.
Jerry Driendl/Getty Images

Right: Night falls over Baltimore and Oriole Park in this 2003 photograph, the out-of-town scoreboard lighting up in the fading light. Babe Ruth was born two blocks from the ballpark 75 years before Oriole Park opened in 1992. The long building past right field is a remnant from the days of the "B&O"—the Baltimore & Ohio Railroad. Built at the turn of the century the warehouse is 1,016 feet long and is used today to house the Orioles' management offices as well as restaurants and bars. The stadium had an electrifying effect on its neighborhood. Architects Populous say that "the year Oriole Park opened, downtown Baltimore spending increased 260 percent. More than 15 years after its opening, Oriole Park's presence was still making an impact; it continues to generate more than $165 million in sales and tax revenues near $10 million per year." Much of the success of the new park has been attributed to its location in the midst of Baltimore's bustling inner harbor (top right).
Roger Miller

Right: Detail of scoreboard from right field: note the B&O warehouse at right and the Emerson Bromo-Seltzer Tower in the distance. Modeled after the Palazzo Vecchio in Florence, Italy, it was completed in 1911 and has been a Baltimore landmark ever since.
Digitalballparks.com

BABE'S DREAM
George Herman "Babe" Ruth
Baltimorean
Feb. 6, 1895 – Aug. 16, 1948

Above: The south end of Eutaw Street enters Camden Yards and runs alongside the stadium's right field affording views of the field of play. In the 2011–2012 off-season the right-field wall was lowered from 25 to 21 feet to improve the view. On game days, the entrance to Eutaw Street is ticketed and when seating is sold out, the street provides some standing room. The street itself is studded with small plaques identifying where home runs have landed. Here it is seen thronging with fans before a game.
Digitalballparks.com

Left: A sculpture of Babe Ruth stands tall outside Oriole Park at Camden Yards. George Herman "Babe" Ruth (1895–1948) was born in Baltimore but started his long career in 1914 with the Boston Red Sox. It was with the Yankees 1920–34 that he came to the fore with prodigious batting feats—54 home runs, then a record, in 1920; 60 in 1927. Among the greatest players baseball has ever seen, he played in 10 World Series, hit 714 home runs (a record that stood until 1974), and was elected to the Hall of Fame in 1936.
Jerry Driendl/Getty Images

Above Right and Right: Two views of Camden Yards on 30 April 2016 prior to a game between the Chicago White Sox and Baltimore Orioles. From the high point of 1997 when attendance was over 3.7 million, the Orioles' attendance figures declined thanks to 14 losing seasons 1998–2011. The wild card berth in 2012 helped, as did another visit to the playoffs in 2014 but it will need continued on-field success to return attendance levels to those of the early 1990s.
Matthew Pintar

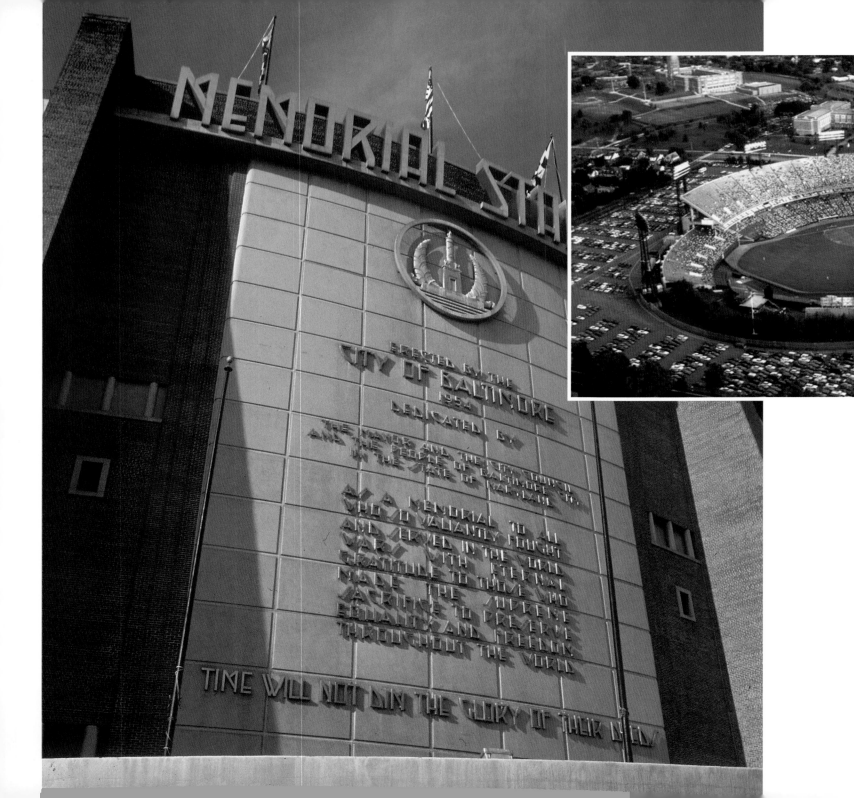

Above and Right: Aerial views of Memorial Stadium, the home of the Orioles until replaced by the new Oriole Park at Camden Yards in 1992. Fans who had loudly voiced their dissatisfaction over the change were soon silenced by the easy access the downtown location provided and the sheer pleasure of watching a game at the new ballpark.
Roger Miller (both)

Left: The "Memorial Wall" at Memorial Stadium was a very large and visible concrete plaque located on the outside of the ballpark behind home plate. Its inscription read: "Dedicated as a memorial to all who so valiantly fought in the world wars with eternal gratitude to those who made the supreme sacrifice to preserve equality and freedom throughout the world—time will not dim the glory of their deeds." Before the stadium was demolished in February 2001, the wall was dismantled and preserved. Parts of it have been incorporated into a new Veteran's Memorial at Oriole Park at Camden Yards.
Roger Miller

MEMORIAL STADIUM
(1954–91)

Home of the Baltimore Orioles Memorial Stadium, like the city it served, was a no frills
place to watch baseball. Originally built for minor league baseball and professional football, an uncovered second deck was added in 1954, when the Browns moved to Baltimore from St. Louis and became the Orioles. Vice President Richard Nixon threw out the ceremonial first pitch on the park's opening day. The park was best known for its meticulous field and devoted fans, many of whom sneered at plans in the early 1990s to replace the worn stadium with a downtown park. Memorial Stadium was home to Brooks Robinson and Frank Robinson, where Jim Palmer, Dave McNally, Pat Dobson, and Mike Cuellar each won 20 games in the same year (1971), where Cal Ripken's iron man streak began, and where Earl Weaver's umpire-arguing, three-runhome- run style of baseball produced champions.

BOSTON RED SOX

FENWAY PARK

Address:
4 Yawkey Way
Boston, MA 02215
Capacity: 37,949
Opening day: April 20, 1912—Boston Red Sox 7, New York Highlanders 6 (11 innings)
Cost to construct: $650,000
Architect: Osborne Engineering Company
Dimensions (ft):
Left Field—310
Left Center—379
Center Field—389
Right Center—380
Right Field—302
Defining feature: Green Monster
Little-known ground rule: A ball going through the Green Monster scoreboard, either on the bound or fly, is two bases
World Series: 1912, 1914, 1918, 1946, 1967, 1975, 1986, 2004, 2007, 2013
All-Star Game: 1946, 1961, 1999
Memorable moments:
1914 July 11—Babe Ruth earns a victory as a pitcher in his major league debut.
1918 September 11—Red Sox win the World Series over the Chicago Cubs.
1975 October 21—Carton Fisk hits a 12th-inning home run off the left field foul pole to win game six of the World Series against the Cincinnati Reds.
2004 October 23—The Sox win the first game of the World Series and go on to lift the "Curse of the Bambino" by beating the Cardinals 4–0.
2013 October 39—38,447 spectators see the Red Sox clinch the World Series at home for the first time since 1918.
2016, October 10—This was the last game for David "Big Papi" Ortiz as the Red Sox were ousted from the playoffs 5-4 by the Cleveland Indians in the American League Division Series.

The Great Wall of China. The Wailing Wall in Jerusalem. The Green Monster in Fenway Park. Few structures in architecture, and none in baseball, are more identifiable than the 37-foot wall that separates Lansdowne Street from the outfield where Duffy Lewis, Ted Williams, and Carl Yazstremski once roamed.

A billboard for the greatness of baseball, the original wall, just 25 feet high, was probably built to keep residents in neighboring apartments from sneaking a free peak at the game. The Green Monster was expanded to its current height in 1934 and painted green in 1947. The seats built on top in 2003 have become among the most prized in baseball.

Fenway, the oldest of today's major league parks, is a living monument to baseball history. Babe Ruth's early pitching days, the Red Sox' dramatic World Series triumph in 1918, Jimmy Foxx and Ted Williams' slugging, Tony Conigliaro's beaning, Carl Yazstremski's left-field mastery, Jim Rice's power, and Pedro Martinez's dominance, make it more than a "little lyrical bandbox of a ballpark," as John Updike famously described it.

Constructed in time for the 1912 season, the new ballpark was named by then Red Sox owner John I. Taylor because it was built in a marshy area of Boston known as the Fens. The opening was pushed off the front pages of Boston newspapers because of the Titanic,

which had sunk just six days earlier. Mayor John F. Fitzgerald threw out the first pitch at the ceremony marking the park's opening, 48 years before his yet-to-be born grandson, John Fitzgerald Kennedy, would win the presidency.

Before the Green Monster there was a steep mound of dirt that rose 10 feet to the left field wall, a fielding nightmare played so masterfully by Red Sox left fielder Duffy Lewis it was nicknamed "Duffy's Cliff."

Fire has repeatedly reshaped baseball's most distinctive park. In 1926, the wooden bleachers along the left-field line burned down, creating an opening that provided fielders a chance to catch foul balls outside the grandstand. Another fire in 1934 convinced the owners to replace wooden stands with concrete. It was post-World War II fire regulations that made the park's capacity, which once approached 48,000, shrink to the lowest of any park in the majors.

The park was also shaped to fit its talent. The bullpens were moved to right field in the 1940s to shorten the fences and take advantage of Williams' left-handed power. A bright red seat in the right field bleachers (Section 42, Row 37, Seat 21) marks the spot of Williams' longest Fenway blast, a 502-foot shot on June 9, 1946, off Fred Hutchinson of the Detroit Tigers.

Today, the base of the left-field wall is anchored by a manual scoreboard, which

not only updates American League scores with 16-inch-high numbers (National League scores are electronic) but features two vertical strips which spell out the initials of former team owners Tom Yawkey and Jean Yawkey—TAY and JRY—in Morse code.

Fenway has been around for most of baseball's history. However it did not witness a Red Sox world championship for many years after its infancy. On the afternoon of September 11, 1918, Les Mann, the Chicago Cubs leftfielder, tapped a ground ball to Sox second baseman Dave Shean, who tossed over to Stuffy McInnis for the out and a 2 to 1 victory. It would take more than eight decades and over 7,000 games before Fenway celebrated another World Series triumph.

At a time when most classic ballparks have been shut down or destroyed, the Red Sox have resisted temptation to move to a new facility, and this was rewarded in 2004 when they defeated the Cardinals to win their first World Series since 1918. Just to prove it was no fluke, they did the same thing in 2007 and, after nearly a century, the 2013 World Series finally saw the ultimate prize: a championship at home.

In late March of 2017, just days before the opening of the new season, the Boston Red Sox showed off some new renovations at venerable Fenway Park, the Major Leagues' oldest ballpark, these came on the heels of a long-term, $285-million renovation

project that spruced up the Grand Old Lady between 2002 and 2011. New investments and improvements put the total spending at over $300 million by 2017.

Dugout renovation is probably the most noticeable—home and visiting teams now enjoy dugouts three feet wider. The park's nearby walls were also moved out by the same three feet which enabled the installation of a few more rows of seating close to the field.

Other renovations include restructuring the Pesky Pole. The Pole, 302 feet down the right-field line from home plate marking the foul line, was named after the legendary former Boston shortstop Johnny Pesky. The 2013 Rooftop Garden was expanded from 5,000 to 5,600 square feet. A virtual reality batting cage in the Kids area was updated. A new video board was installed in right field replacing a sponsor sign.

Before the season, the Red Sox announced they would retire the No. 34 jersey number of David Ortiz on June 23, 2017. Ortiz concluded his 20-year career in 2016 with 541 home runs.

Right: Postwar aerial view of Fenway Park before the extensive modifications to the stands. Note no bleachers on top of the Green Monster; these were added before the 2003 season.
National Baseball Hall of Fame

Left: A view outside Fenway Park as fans arrive for the game between the Red Sox and the Yankees on July 25, 2003. Three World Series victories in the last 15 years and regular postseason appearances help keep the Fenway seats full. Usually in the top five best-attended MLB ballparks, the annual figure hovers around three million.
Jerry Driendl/Getty Images

Right: Panoramic interior view of Fenway Park from the seats above first base during the July 25, 2003 Red Sox-Yankees game. Note the bleachers atop the Green Monster. Since the arrival of the new millennium there were ten years of renovations and improvements including three new HD video display and scoring systems, improved waterproofing, seat replacements, and a number of new features such as the new Home Plate Deck.
Jerry Driendl/Getty Images

Right: Mounted police on crowd control outside Fenway Park in 1912. *National Baseball Hall of Fame*

Far Right: A similar view to the last photograph. This one, some 40 years later, is a postwar view of Fenway Park that shows some of the building that had taken place since 1912. *National Baseball Hall of Fame*

Left: Fenway Park during the All-Star Game on June 30, 1999. It was just after the start of 1947 that workers started to install light towers at Fenway Park, allowing night games for the first time. The other major change for the 1947 season was the cleaning up of the left-field wall. All the advertisements were removed and the wall was painted green, thus creating the "Green Monster," such a defining feature of the ballpark. The photograph also highlights one of the problems with older ballparks: obstructed views by the 26 poles that hold the upper-deck up. From a very few seats, neither batter's nor pitcher's mound can be seen.
Getty Images

Right: Aerial view from the Prudential Tower, May 1, 2012. At right edge of photo the Massachusetts Turnpike. In the foreground, the greenery of the Back Bay Fens, designed by Frederick Law Olmsted as part of Boston's Emerald Necklace of parks.
WonderWhy via WikiCommons (CC BY-SA 3.0)

NEW YORK YANKEES

NEW YANKEE STADIUM

Address:
East 161st Street and River Ave.
Bronx, NY 10452
Capacity: 54,251
Opening day: April 16, 2009—Cleveland 10, New York Yankees 2
Cost to construct: $1.5 billion
Architect: Populous
Dimensions (ft): these are as the old Yankee stadium
Left Field—318
Left Center—399
Center Field—408
Right Center—385
Right Field—314
Defining feature: Reinstating the distinctive copper frieze that lined the old stadium
Little-known ground rule: A ball hitting the foul pole in the 1930s was in play, not a homer
World Series: in the old stadium—1923, 1926–28, 1932, 1936–39, 1941–43, 1947, 1949–53, 1955–58, 1960–64, 1976–78, 1981, 1996, 1998–2001, 2003; in the new stadium—2009
All-Star Game: in the old stadium—1939, 1960, 1977, 2008
Memorable moments:

2009 October 7—The new stadium's first playoff game sees the Yankees defeat the Twins thanks to two-run homers by Derek Jeter and Hideki Matsui.

2009 October 25—The Yankees win their first ALCS pennant since 2003 by beating the Angels 4–2

2009 November 4—The Yankees make their 40th World Series appearance, defeating the Phillies 7–3 on the night and 4–2. Andy Pettitte makes it a career total of 18 playoff wins.

2013 April 12—The Yankees make their second-ever triple play in a home game against the Baltimore Orioles.

2017, May 14—Long-time star shortstop Derek Jeter's No. 2 jersey was retired.

Few structures house more American memories than the old Yankee Stadium that was demolished at the end of the 2008 stadium. Ruth, Gehrig, DiMaggio, and Mantle are among the legends that have made history on these 10 acres in the South Bronx. Opened during the Harding presidency and still filling seats many presidents later, the majestic, structure has hosted heavyweight championships, football games, international soccer matches, world leaders, two popes, Bruce Springsteen, and Pink Floyd.

Yankee Stadium became synonymous with the most successful sports franchise in America, hosting the World Series nearly every other year since it opened—so it was no real surprise when the new stadium opened to another World Series victory.

America was dotted with ballparks in 1923, when the Yankees opened the first baseball field to be dubbed a "stadium." Like the team that called it home, there was nothing modest or understated about its confines. Three decks of grandstands, originally intended to encircle the park to deprive non-paying bystanders a free look, rose above home plate, with a distinctive copper frieze decorating the roof of the top deck.

Babe Ruth himself, a left-handed hitter who is responsible for the short right field porch, hit the park's first home run to the roaring approval of the New York faithful, who quickly called it "the house that Ruth built."

It was here, just across the Harlem River from the Polo Grounds (which the Giants and even the Yankees once called home), that Joe McCarthy and Casey Stengel managed the Yankees to a combined 18 pennants, where Ruth hit his 60th and where Roger Maris hit No. 61. It was the home to Murderer's row, the Iron Horse, the Yankee Clipper, and the "Straw that stirs the drink."

Cemetery-sized monuments to Manager Miller Huggins and later Gehrig and Ruth were placed in deep center field, 10 feet from the wall. Patrons could pay homage to their heroes as they exited through the center field gate, and watch as balls hit sharply to center field occasionally rattled around gravestone-looking monuments. Plaques to DiMaggio and Mantle were also added in 1969.

The legends were not limited to baseball. It was here on a cold November day in 1928, that Notre Dame coach Knute Rockne, facing an undefeated Army team, asked his players to "win one for the Gipper," which they did on a pair of second half touchdowns. It was here that the Baltimore Colts defeated the New York Giants in sudden death during the 1958 NFL championship, regarded as "the greatest game ever played." Joe Louis claimed the heavyweight championship of the world here. Pele scored goals. Pope Paul VI delivered mass in 1965, and Pope John Paul II did the same 14 years later.

Decades of use necessitated major renovations, and for the 1974 and 197_ seasons the Yankees played at Shea Stadiu_ as their stadium underwent reconstructio_ costing at least 25 times more than the origin_ park. The new stadium met mixed review_ The copper frieze was replaced by plasti_ the monuments in center field were move_ beyond the outfield walls. Some complaine_ that a baseball relic had been turned in_ another cookie-cutter design. Nonetheles_ the upgrade added at least three decades _ the stadium's life, which ended with the 200_ season.

The new Yankee Stadium was built rig_ next door and was ready for play in Ap_ 2009. The ground-breaking ceremony _ August 16, 2006, very neatly coincided wi_ the anniversary of Babe Ruth's death. Much _ the new stadium provides a sense of continui_ and echoes the old: a triumphal entrance, th_ limestone and granite outer wall, the field _ dimensions, the location of the bullpen _ Monument Park moved to the new stadium_ center field wall—and the reinstating of th_ distinctive copper frieze that lined the ol_ stadium until 1973. The new stadium boas_ more legroom than the old; 56 luxury suite_ rather than 19; a bigger scoreboard, the Ne_ York Yankees Museum more retail outlet_ and generally better amenities—but highe_ prices and fans' reactions have been mixed.

Success in the first season—including 8_ home runs in the first 23 games and a Worl_

Left and Below: The similarities between the frontages of the new and old Yankee Stadiums are marked. Here they are seen in their opening years, 2009 for the new stadium and opening day, April 18, 1923, for the old. *BuickCenturyDriver via WikiCommons; National Baseball Hall of Fame*

Series victory over the Phillies—have given the stadium a fantastic start.

All the improvements have made Yankee Stadium the most expensive stadium ever built. To capitalize on the improvements, the stadium is also used as a venue for rock concerts and other sporting events. Most notably, since 2012 it has hosted regular soccer matches, and as of 2015 New York City FC, an MLS expansion team, is using the stadium until their new home is completed.

Although the "new" Yankee Stadium was beginning just its ninth season of operation for the 2017 season, the Yankees announced some ballpark improvements. For the first time a Yankee Stadium offered a children's special area. The Sunrun Kids Clubhouse includes a playground and a small baseball field. Also, the stadium added more concessions stands around the park.

Left: Great ground-level view inside the new Yankee Stadium. Note the frieze around the top of the upper deck that recaptures the original stadium's grandeur, and the scoreboard. The 103-by-58-foot, HD Mitsubishi Diamond Vision LED display is six times larger than the screen at old Yankee Stadium.
Alex Jagendorf

Above and Right: The frieze around the new stadium harks back to the decorative cast-iron work on the roof edge of the old stadium. It was made of copper but painted white in the 1960s. It was removed in the 1970s while extra seating was being added to the upper deck. This would be echoed on the New Yankee Stadium, with a similar frieze made of steel painted white. Photo at right taken in 1947 during the World Series between the Yankees and the Dodgers. At left, the view on May 24, 2009. *Associated Press/National Baseball Hall of Fame (right); Y2kcrazyjoker4 via WikiCommons (CC BY 3.0)*

Left: This 2010 aerial view shows the footprint of the demolished stadium at left—today it's a part of Macombs Dam Park which includes softball, baseball, and Little League grass fields as well as the Joseph Yancey Track and Field, a running track that surrounds an all-weather soccer or football surface. The green-blue roofs of 161st Street station are in the center of the photo. *Gryffindor via WikiCommons (CC BY-SA 3.0)*

Left: Yankee Stadium seen from across the river at dusk during the Mets-Yankees game on June 27, 2003.
Jerry Driendl/Getty Images

Left and Far Left: Two aerial views of Yankee Stadium. The first (left) was taken on September 9, 1928 and shows the Yankees playing the Phillies. The second photograph (far left) shows a 1960s view. Note the proximity of the New York City Transit's subway system: the 161st Street station (at center top of photo) today handles over 8 million passengers a year—the record is 8.8 million in 2012.
National Baseball Hall of Fame

Following page, Left: The old Yankee Stadium during the game against the Texas Rangers on April 12, 2000. On-field success— six World Series appearances between 1996 and 2003pushed up attendances to over 4 million, peaking at 4,298,655 in 2008, ironically their worst season for 15 years. Another World Series win in 2009 and regular playoff positions have kept attendances well over three million since then in the new stadium.
Al BelloAllsport via Getty Images

Following page, Right: An exterior view of the old stadium and its proud declaration of the 26 World Championships won there. The structure in the shape of a baseball bat was erected in front of the stadium in 1976. For fans, it was a popular meeting point. Its real function was to serve as an exhaust chimney for the stadium's boilers. The design was modeled after a Louisville Slugger, just like that used by Yankee Sluggers to win those 26 World Championships.
National Baseball Hall of Fame

TAMPA BAY RAYS

TROPICANA FIELD

Address:
One Tropicana Drive
St. Petersburg, FL 33705
Capacity: 42,735
Opening day: March 31, 1998—Detroit Tigers 11,
Tampa Bay Devil Rays 6
Cost to construct: $138 million
Architect: HOK Sport; Lescher & Mahoney Sports
Dimensions (ft):
Left Field—315
Left Center—370
Center Field—404
Right Center—370
Right Field—322
Defining feature: Left Field "beach"
Little-known ground rule: A batted ball that hits either
of the lower two catwalks, lights, or suspended objects
in fair territory is a home run
World Series: 2008
All-Star Game: none
Memorable moments:
1999 May 2—Jose Canseco hits a towering blast onto a
catwalk. When the ball doesn't come down, he is
awarded a double.
1999 August 7—Wade Boggs gets his 3,000th hit, a
home run.
2000 September 17—Devil Rays game with the Oakland
Athletics is postponed because of Hurricane
Gordon, only the third domed game ever
postponed by weather.
2008 October 11—The Rays win game 2 of the ALCS in
the eleventh after 5 hours and 27 minutes of play.
2008 October 19—The Rays beat the Red Sox 3–1 to
take the AL Championship in front of 40,743.
2008 October 23—The Rays defeat the Phillies 4–2 to
win game 2 of the World Series but lose the next
three.

If you build it, they will come. That was the hope of stadium investors and Florida baseball fans when the Florida Suncoast Dome (as it was then known) was completed in 1986. The state-of-the-art stadium had everything a modern park needed except a team. Business leaders tried to lure the White Sox, the Twins, and the Expos, but failed. A local businessman even purchased the San Francisco Giants for $113 million, but major league owners rejected the move. ("No team should be able to move nilly-willy," said Texas Ranger managing partner George W. Bush at the time.)

Major League Baseball finally rewarded Florida's baseball-starved fans the expansion Devil Rays in 1996, after owners agreed to spend $85 million to convert what had become known as the Thunderdome, home of the NHL Lightnings, into a baseball haven.

Purists frown on domed stadiums. Nevertheless, Tropicana Field, as it was named when it reopened, was made exclusively for baseball. Inspired by Ebbets Field, a grand, eight-story high rotunda greets fans as they enter. The asymmetrical outfield dimensions closely match those from the old Brooklyn Dodger home. Seats are just 50 feet behind home plate, among the closest in the majors. To mimic the look of an outdoor stadium, the field features all-dirt base paths on artificial turf, the first major-league park to do so since St. Louis' Busch Stadium two decades earlier.

Dubbed "the Ballpark of the 21st Century" by team owner Vince Naimoli the year it opened, the stadium is loaded with amenities. The main rotunda features 1.8 million color tiles and a sound system delivering play-by-play of memorable baseball moments. The Center Field Street includes a cigar bar and restaurant, a billiards hall, a brew house, and a climbing wall. A restaurant in the batter's line of vision in dead center field is aptly named the "Batter's Eye." An area known as "The Beach" in left field's second deck features palm trees, a spa, a restaurant, and ushers dressed in Hawaiian shirts. A Rays' home victory is announced to the outside by lighting the roof of Tropicana Field orange.

Tropicana Field has the world's second-largest cable-supported domed roof (after the Georgia Dome in Atlanta). The Teflon-coated fiberglass slants at a distinct angle. With hurricanes in mind, the roof is built to withstand wind up to 115 miles per hour. A versatile park, the stadium has hosted 16 other sports, including sprint car and motorcycle racing, gymnastics, tennis, weight-lifting, karate, motorcycle racing, equestrian events, track, figure skating, and ping pong.

There was a further $25-million facelift prior to the 2006 season; $10 million was spent on improvements during the same season; and further improvements were made in the offseason before the 2007 season.

In 2007 the Devil Rays dropped the Devil from their title and became the Rays. The results were immediate! In 2008 they reached the World Series, a great achievement although they lost 4–1 to the Phillies.

Tropicana Field is the only Major League ballpark to feature an artificial surface—new AstroTurf was installed prior to the 2011 season, and all-dirt base paths.

The Tampa Bay Rays are contracted to stay at Tropicana Field until 2027, but in 2015 the city council ruled they could leave earlier if they pay a $5 million demolition charge plus $4 million a year for every early year vacated. At a cost of $1 million, Tropicana Field installed a new artificial turf surface on the field under the roof for the 2017 season. Hailing the turf as the best in the business, team officials expect it to provide truer bounces on ground balls.

The Rays also shopped for a new chef to oversee food operations. A variety of new concessions stands were added to the menu, as was a featured item called the $16 "Brunch Bloody Mary" which is essentially a meal in a glass. It is a skewer of chicken, sausage, waffles, donuts, egg and bacon towering above a plastic keeper mason jar.

Right: Inside the dome of Tropicana Field, home of the Tampa Bay Rays since 1998.
Digitalballparks.com

Left: Palm trees flank the entrance to Tropicana Field. Named after a rights deal with Tropicana Dole Beverages North America, the Rays' website identifies 16 other sports and competitions presented in the facility including hockey, basketball, football, sprint car racing, gymnastics, soccer, tennis, weightlifting, karate, motorcycle racing, equestrian events, table tennis, track and figure skating. However, the largest crowd to date—47,150—was for the August 11, 1990, concert featuring The New Kids on the Block.
Digitalballparks.com

Above: The Tropicana Field dome from the air on September 15, 2009.
Opakapaka via WikiCommons

Left: Tropicana left field from the upper deck. It's not the best ballpark in MLB. As Joe Mock of baseball.com said: "The Trop is a bad facility in a bad location." The attendance figures bear this out: half way through the 2014 season the Rays were being watched by an average of under 18,000—only Cleveland was worse. Even in their World Series year the total attendance was only 1.8 million.
Digitalballparks.com

TORONTO BLUE JAYS

ROGERS CENTRE

Aka: SkyDome (1989–2005)
Address:
One Blue Jays Way Suite 3200
Toronto, Ontario M5V 1J1
Capacity: 53,506
Opening day: June 5, 1989—Milwaukee Brewers 5, Toronto Blue Jays 3
Cost to construct: $500 million
Architect: Rod Robbie and Michael Allen
Dimensions (ft):
Left Field—328
Left Center—375
Center Field—400
Right Center—375
Right Field—328
Defining feature: Retractable dome
Little-known ground rule: Whether a game begins with the roof open or closed depends on the Toronto Blue Jays. If the game begins with the roof closed: It shall not be opened at any time during the game.
World Series: 1992, 1993
All-Star Game: 1991
Memorable moments:
1989 October 7—Oakland's Jose Canseco hits a 500-plus foot home run into the fifth deck during game four of the league championship series.
1993 October 23—Joe Carter's ninth-inning, three-run homer to the left field seats wins the World Series over Philly 8–6 for Toronto's second consecutive world championship.
1998 July 5—Roger Clemens records his 3,000th career strikeout.
2014 August 10—Jays win the longest game in franchise history in time and innings: 6 hours, 37 minutes, winning 6–5 in 19 innings against the Tigers.
2015 October 19—An 11–8 victory over Kansas City gives the Jays their first playoff victory since 1993.
2016 September 29—The Rogers Centre attendance total of 3,392,099 was the playoff-bound Blue Jays' highest since 1993.

Baseball has always been afraid of the elements, suffering through cold springs and canceling games in the rain. And then came SkyDome.

With its retractable roof, the first for any sports arena in the world, engineers figured out how to make baseball playable from April though October, even in the frigid north. Balancing 22 million tons 31 stories in the sky, SkyDome takes 20 minutes to open or close its four rooftop panels, which cover 340,000 square feet.

When it is open, downtown's trademark CN Tower looms over right field, and the downdraft makes home runs difficult. When it is closed, the dome is among the tallest in the majors, and the park turns into a hitter's field.

The perfectly symmetrical SkyDome was state-of-the-art when it opened, just six years before quirky Camden Yards would touch off a revival of uniquely shaped ballparks. The pitchers' mound is constructed on a fiberglass dish which allows it to be raised or lowered by hydraulics, and eight miles of zippers connect the strips of artificial turf.

Home to the Canadian Football League's Toronto Argonauts, SkyDome is much more than just baseball. The building contains a huge 348-room Renaissance Hotel, with 70 rooms overlooking the playing field (where guests have exposed themselves in compromising positions more than once), a Hard Rock Cafe, a 300-foot bar with all seats facing the field, a health club with squash courts, a mini-golf course, and an indoor running track.

As much an architectural attraction as a sports venue, SkyDome was the first major-league park to exceed four million patrons in a single season, a feat it accomplished three years in a row. The stadium's $17 million, 33-foot by 110-foot Jumbotron video scoreboard with its 67,200 light bulbs is North America's largest.

The name SkyDome (not the SkyDome) was the result of a contest, selected from among 12,879 entries. The winner, Kellie Watson, was asked by the *Toronto Globe and Mail* to explain the name.

"It was dome," she responded, "where you could see the sky."

The SkyDome is now called Rogers Centre, honoring Rogers Communications, which now owns both the stadium and the Blue Jays. Following the demise of the Montreal Expos in 2004 and their reemergence as the Washington Nationals, the Toronto Blue Jays became Canada's only major league baseball team.

The 1992 and 1993 Blue Jays took back-to-back World Series titles, knocking off the Braves and Phillies, respectively. Since those glory years success has eluded the team, and there had been no return trips to the playoffs until the Jays reached the ALCS in 2015.

Known for its cheap tickets, bland concrete expanses, and fantastic retracting roof, the SkyDome (because that's what fans will always call it) has all the drawbacks of a multi-sport stadium—and all the benefits of a downtown location. However, for the future the stadium urgently needs renovating and updating at an estimated cost of $250 million. These plans include the installation of a natural grass playing field by 2018.

The ballpark once known as SkyDome renovated its "sky" during the off-season, thus completing a $10 million upgrade of the roof.

Although no replacement of the 1989 ballpark is contemplated, the Blue Jays are planning a long-term overhaul of the facilities. The team intended to reveal the outline of that broader renovation by the end of 2017.

Right: The Rogers Centre viewed from the CN Tower on August 5, 2009. SkyDome until 2005, for the 2015 Pan American Games it was renamed the Pan Am Dome and hosted the opening and closing ceremonies.
Rrburke via WikiCommons (CC BY-SA 3.0)

Above and Above Right:
Two details of SkyDome.
With the roof open, the
downdraft from the tower
makes batting a much more
difficult job than when it's
closed.
Digitalballparks.com

Right: An August 2005
view—midway through an
over-20-year run without
reaching the playoffs, the
Jays still mustered over two
million fans in 2005. In 2015
that jumped to nearly 2.8
million thanks to a 93–63
winning season when they
took the AL East crown.
*Minestrone via
WikiCommons*

Opposite, Above Left:
Game 2 of the 1993 World
Series between the Blue Jays
and the Philadelphia Phillies
on October 17. It ended a
6–4 win for the Phillies. Six
days later Joe Carter won the
sixth game, and the series,
with a three-run homer. He
had, the year before, caught
the final out as first baseman.
*Rick Stewart/Allsport via
Getty Images*

Opposite, Above Right: The
exterior of the Rogers Centre
on September 10, 2008.
*Taxiarchos228 via Wikipedia
(CC BY-SA 3.0)*

Left: Inside SkyDome with the roof open; photo taken in 1989. There have been many changes to the stadium since this photo was taken, mainly since Rogers Communications bought SkyDome for $25 million in January 2000. The main video board was upgraded from a Jumbotron to a modern Daktronics board in 2005. A center-field porch was added to the 200 level in 2013, the same year that Paul Beeston, President of the Blue Jays, said that the stadium needed $250 million in renovations. Surrounding the main scoreboard are the 70 rooms in the adjoining Renaissance Hotel that afford views of the playing area.
Rick Stewart/Allsport via Getty Images

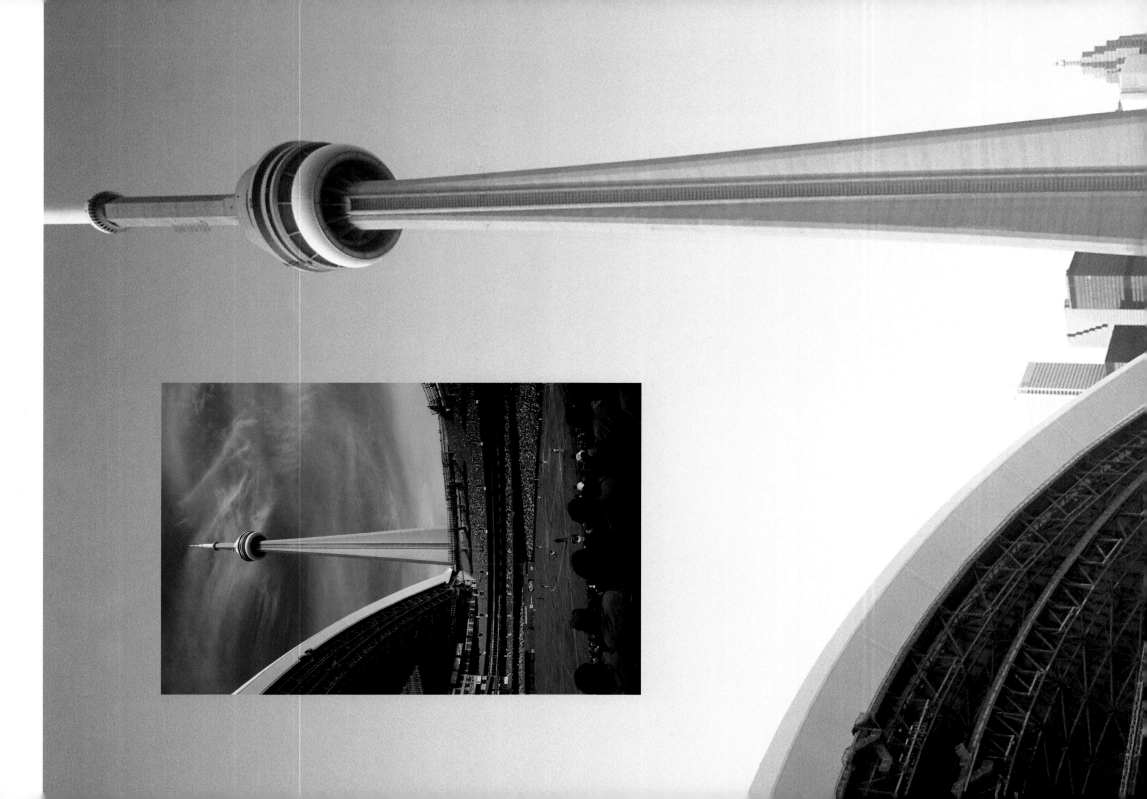

Left: Toronto's CN Tower rises over SkyDome—creating real problems for sluggers. When the roof is open, over 90 percent of the seats and the entire field is open to the sky, an area of 3.2 hectares (7.9 acres).
Nik Wheeler/Corbis

Inset: Photo taken during the last Jays' game of 2007. Third in the league with an 83–79 record, it was another mediocre season.
Re-stitched using Hugin by Nicolas Sanchez MarcusObal via WikiCommons (CC BY-SA 3.0)

They had the best of parks. They had the worst of parks. The ballfields that have been used by the American League Central Division included Cleveland's Progressive Field, so lovely it sold out 455 consecutive games, and Minnesota's Hubert H. Humphrey Metrodome, a baseball design so hideous that even Twins fans demanded its demolition.

Today, the American League Central Division includes one park from the 1970s, two from the 1990s, and two from the 2000s. Though each offers its unique charms, Progressive Field, Detroit's Comerica Park, and Kansas City's Kauffman Stadium are all regarded as wonderful places to watch a baseball game. Chicago's U.S. Cellular Field—opened just a year before Baltimore's Camden Yards would incite a demand for old-fashioned retro-parks—is functional. And Minnesota's Hubert H. Humphrey Metrodome, with its dim lighting, its hefty bag outfield, and its bright, ball-losing, Teflon ceiling was barely that. The Twins finally managed to move in 2010—to the purpose-built Target Field. What a difference! But the lack of a roof could sure be interesting in Minnesota's cooler periods. The rest of the parks of the Central Division should be around for a while, although attendances are languishing at the Indians (down two million from the 1990s), White Sox (down a million since winning the World Series in 2005), and the Twins (a million down since 2010). The Tigers, who missed the playoffs in 2015 for the first time in five years, were still within spitting distance of three million, and the Royals enjoyed an extra million visitors after back-to-back World Series in 2014 and 2015 culminating in their 4–1 mauling of the Mets in 2015.

U.S. Cellular Field from home plate upper level during the game between the Cleveland Indians and the White Sox on June 21, 2003. *Jerry Driendl/Getty Images*

CHICAGO WHITE SOX

GUARANTEED RATE FIELD

Aka: Comiskey Park 1991–2002; Guaranteed Rate Field

Address:
333 West 35th St.
Chicago, Ill 60616

Capacity: 40,615

Opening day: April 18, 1991—Detroit Tigers 16, Chicago White Sox 0

Cost to construct: $167 million

Architect: HOK Sport

Dimensions (ft):
Left Field—330
Left Center—377
Center Field—400
Right Center—372
Right Field—335

Defining feature: Exploding scoreboard

Little-known ground rule: Any fair, batted ball that travels over the yellow line painted on the outfield fence is a home run

World Series: 2005

All-Star Game: 2003

Memorable moments:

1993 April 9—Bo Jackson homers on his first major-league swing.

1993 June 22—Carlton Fisk catches his 2,226th game, a major-league record.

1997 June 16—The Cubs beat the White Sox 8–3 in Chicago's first regular season hometown matchup. The Sox come back to win the next two.

1998 July 31—Albert Belle establishes a major-league record by hitting his 16th home run of the month.

2002 September 19—Father and son spectators run onto field and attack Royals first base coach Tom Gamboa.

2005 October 2—The White Sox beat the Astros 6–7 to take a 2–0 lead in the World Series. They go on to win 4–0.

2008—The White Sox set a new season's home record at Cellular Field of 54–28.

The White Sox home was built under duress. Team owner Jerry Reinsdorf had issued the city an ultimatum: build a new ballpark or he'd take the team to Florida. The Illinois legislature resisted, but eventually agreed to build a park directly across the street from 80-year-old Comiskey Park, which Shoeless Joe Jackson and Luke Appling once called home and where Bill Veeck introduced the world to an exploding scoreboard and disco demolition night.

The new stadium saved baseball for Chicago's South Side. It also produced one of the most maligned ballparks of the modern era. Completed just one year before Camden Yards brought baseball back to the future, the park does not include many of the touches that have made new ballparks instant classics.

There is little inside to let you know that you are in one of America's great baseball cities. The field is almost exactly symmetrical. The top deck is far from the field, and rises at a harrowingly steep slope in order to expose the lower deck to the sky and make room for two tiers of money-making luxury boxes. How distant is the top deck? The front row of upper deck seats is further from the playing field than the back row at the Old Comiskey. Heavy winds off Lake Michigan have closed the upper deck on a few occasions for the safety of the fans.

Still, it was the first park built exclusively for baseball since Kansas City's Kauffman Stadium in 1973. Unlike its predecessor, there are wide concourses, lots of amenities, and no obstructed-view seats. The owners built a new exploding scoreboard, with pinwheels and fireworks set off by a White Sox home run. The uniforms of eight retired players are displayed there: Luke Appling (4), Nellie Fox (2), Minnie Minoso (9), Luis Aparicio (11), Ted Lyons (16), Billy Pierce (19), Carlton Fisk (72), and Harold Baines (3).

In its first year, the reviews were not so bad, and 2,934,154 fans shattered the club's attendance record. But when Camden Yards opened the following year fans began to realize what they had lost out on in Chicago.

The White Sox sold the naming rights to U.S. Cellular for 20 years at a price of $68 million in 2003, depriving baseball of one of its best known names (for all of his playing, managing, and owning days, what Charlie Comiskey is best remembered for is his stinginess toward his players that contributed to the "Black Sox" scandal of 1919.) The club has pledged to spend generously on stadium renovations. The fences have been moved in, a huge high-resolution video screen has been installed in the scoreboard, and a new fan deck, which allows fans to peer over the outfield from above the batter's line of vision in center field, has been added.

Just like old Comiskey, U.S. Cellular Field is a looming fixture on the Dan Ryan Expressway. For nearly two years, the two stadiums stood side-by-side, monuments to the past and the future, before wrecking balls did away with the past.

Regular improvements have been made to the stadium and facilities: between 2001–2007 large scale renovations were completed including improving the bullpens, increasing the seating, new scoreboards and video boards, and improving the concourse and public areas. Three new HD video boards were installed for the start of the 2016 season.

When the White Sox opened a new ballpark in 1991, it was regarded as the second coming of Comiskey Park, the team's main field for decades. Comiskey Park was named after former owner Charles Comiskey. That stadium opened in 1910 and operated through the 1990 season.

Starting in 1991, when the new park opened next-door, the original park became known in conversation as "Old Comiskey." However, the new park was then renamed U.S. Cellular Field for a 20-year period. The deal was extended, but after the 2016 season, Guaranteed Rate, a mortgage company, purchased the naming rights of the facility for 13 years.

The latest renovation in the ballpark came in 2016 and consisted of three new HD video boards, one each in right field, left field, and center field.

Left: For 80 years, until 1990, the home of the Chicago White Sox, Comiskey Park was also home to many baseball greats, among them Shoeless Joe Jackson, Luke Appling, Nellie Fox, Minnie Minoso, and Luis Aparicio. The era of Bill Veeck's ownership, which began in 1959, saw such innovations as the "exploding" scoreboard, player names on the back of team jerseys, and special promotional events such as the disastrous Disco Demolition Night.
National Baseball Hall of Fame

COMISKEY PARK
(1910–90)
Home of the Chicago White Sox.

Comiskey Park opened just a few years before todays surviving gems: Wrigley Field, Fenway Park, and Yankee Stadium. Comiskey was a much larger park, built to create long runs for outfielders and thrilling extra-base hits, rather than uncontested home runs. Pitchers loved it. The park was home to baseball's first All-Star game in 1933. In 1960, Bill Veeck rigged the scoreboard to explode after every White Sox home run, a Comiskey tradition that continues today. Another promotion in 1979 didn't work out so well. Veeck invited fans to Disco Demolition Night, charging just 98 cents for bleacher fans who brought disco records to burn between doubleheader games. The outfield inferno resulted in 50 arrests, and White Sox were forced to forfeit the second game.

Above: The exterior of Old Comiskey Park in 1986, four years before its last MLB game and five before its demolition when it was the oldest park in use by MLB.
Johnmaxmena2 via WikiCommons

Right: A view from the press box at Comiskey Park during the 1959 World Series. The White Sox lost to the Dodgers 4–2. It wouldn't be until 2005 that the Sox had another chance to win a World Series: they took that one 4–0.
Time Life Pictures/Getty Images

Far Right: The new owner of the Chicago White Sox, Bill Veeck, standing in a snowy Comiskey Park. Veeck (1914–1986) was one of the great men of postwar baseball, at various times the owner of the Cleveland Indians, St. Louis Browns, and Chicago White Sox. He was also instrumental in breaking the color bar in baseball, signing Larry Doby for Cleveland. Doby was the first black player in the American League and was followed the next year, 1948, by Satchel Paige. Veeck had two spells with the White Sox; first, 1959–1961 during which he introduced the first "exploding scoreboard." The second was 1975–1981 during which the extreme Disco Demolition Night attracted a huge crowd but led to the forfeiture of the next day's game against the Tigers, the last game to have been won by forfeit in the American League.
Time Life Pictures/Getty Images

Guaranteed Rate Field on May 13, 2017.
as 29,111 fans watch the Chicago White Sox play
the San Diego Padres. *Ron Vesely/MLB Photos via
Getty Images*

Right: Exterior of U.S. Cellular Field in June 2003. Until the naming rights were sold that year, the ballpark had been called Comiskey Park.
Jerry Driendl/Getty Images

Following page: This September 2013 view of U.S. Cellular Field was taken from the bleachers of Section 164 during a White Sox–Tigers game. The first big stadium built in Chicago since the 1920s, it has seen a number of renovations since the turn of the millennium.
Mr. Konerko via WikiCommons (CC BY-SA 3.0)

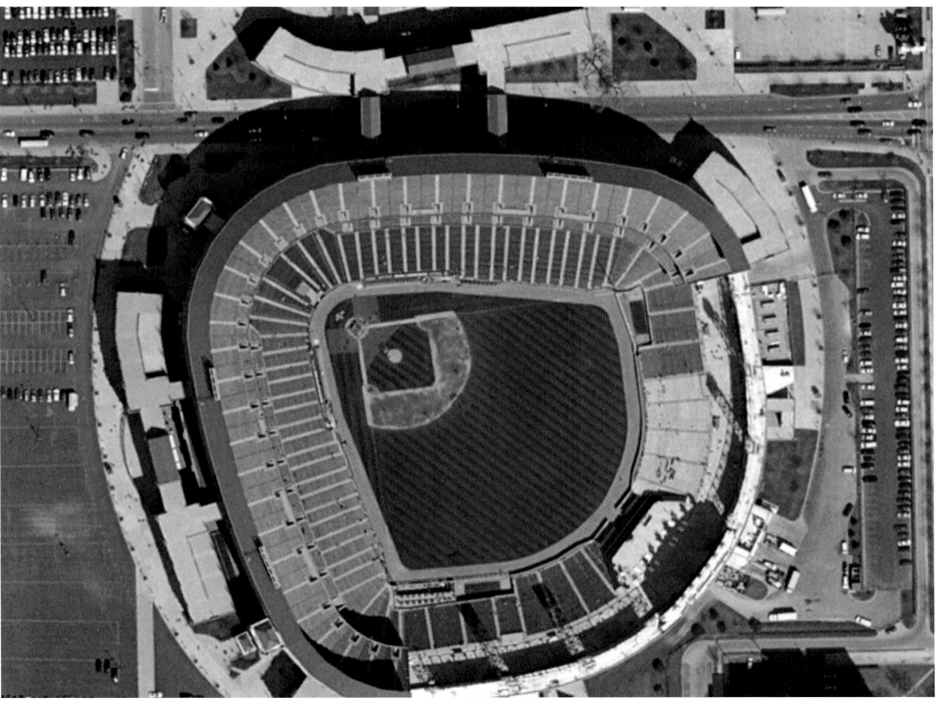

Far Left: A July 23, 1995, view of the new Comiskey Park that shows off the height of the upper level. Intended to improve sightlines, the height was not universally admired. *Jonathan Daniel/Allsport via Getty Images*

Left: A satellite view of U.S. Cellular Field, showing I-94 and the Dan Ryan Expressway to the right of the photo and W35th Street running along the top side of the ballpark. Since the start of the 2017 season the ballpark has been called Guaranteed Rate Field. *USGS via WikiCommons*

CLEVELAND INDIANS

PROGRESSIVE FIELD

Aka: Jacobs Field 1994–2008
Address:
2401 Ontario Street
Cleveland, OH 44115
Capacity: 35,225
Opening day: April 4, 1994—Cleveland Indians 4, Kansas City 3 (11 innings)
Cost to construct: $175 million
Architect: HOK Sports
Dimensions (ft):
Left Field—325
Left Center—370
Center Field—405
Right Center—375
Right Field—325
Defining feature: Left field scoreboard
Little-known ground rule: Thrown ball that enters camera pits, dugouts, or diamond suites and remains: two bases
World Series: 1995, 1997, 2016
All-Star Game: 1997
Memorable moments:
1994 April 4—Wayne Kirby's 11th-inning single gives Cleveland a 4–3 victory in the Jake's debut.
1995 September 8—Cleveland defeats Baltimore 3–2 to clinch the AL Central Division, its first championship in 41 years.
2001 August 5—Trailing the Mariners 14–2, the Tribe scores 13 unanswered runs for their greatest comeback in 76 years.
2012 April 5—A record crowd of 43,190 watch the longest opening day game in MLB history: 16 innings over 5 hours and 14 minutes against the Toronto Blue Jays. The Indians lose 7–4.
2016, June 17-July 1—The Indians won a team-record 14 straight games.
2016, October 25—Game 1 of the World Series between the Indians and Chicago Cubs concluded with a 6-0 Cleveland victory in the team's first appearance in the Series since 1997.

They serve pierogies and sushi at the Jake. After playing for 61 years at cavernous Municipal Stadium at the edge of Lake Erie, derisively labeled the "mistake by the lake," the Indians moved into a boutique park where the blend of old and new is among the wonders of modern baseball.

Where the old stadium looked like something a child would build with an advanced erecter set, Jacobs Field was carefully sculpted to blend Indians' baseball with Cleveland's industrial roots.

The architects boast of using the city's traditional stone and brick masonry and providing direct views into the park from two street-level plazas to further integrate it with the city. Critics have credited the latticework on the exterior for reflecting the bridges that cross the Cuyahoga River and the light standards for mimicking the industrial city's smokestacks. The result is an urban structure that is an integral part of Cleveland's downtown renaissance.

While the old stadium offered little more than a baseball diamond and seats, the Jake is a feast for the eyes. An appealing panorama of downtown Cleveland—if such a thing is possible—rises over the outfield, as does a 120-foot tall, 222-foot wide scoreboard, at the time boasting to be the largest freestanding scoreboard in the majors. The left-field scoreboard is reachable only by the likes of Mark McGwire, who did it off Orel Hershiser on April 30, 1997. Seats are angled to face the action at the plate.

Some elements resemble other parks. The 19-foot tall left-field fence, is referred to as the "mini-green monster." The bleachers compare to Wrigley's. Like most old parks, the playing field is anything but symmetric. Dead center field is not as deep as deepest left center. There is a triple deck in right. Home plate was transplanted from the old Municipal Stadium.

The new park is named after Richard Jacobs, who bought the Indians in 1985 and paid for the stadium's naming rights. The new home has suited the Indians well. Perennial losers, the Tribe won five consecutive division titles from 1995 to 1999. The stadium was sold out for an astounding record of 455 consecutive games, which would have been unimaginable at its old home.

Hitter-friendly Progressive Field was renamed after a local insurance company in 2008. It is one of the most attractive ballparks in Major League Baseball, offering spectacular views of downtown Cleveland. In 2008 readers of *Sports Illustrated* voted it the most beautiful. Architects HOK Sport, produced a design that included exposed steelwork to reflect the area's many bridges, and towers that echoed the city's smokestacks and skyscrapers.

Poor performances mean that attendance has been patchy of late. Half way through the 2014 season the Indians had attracted an average of just over 15,000 to their games giving a running total under a third of the top team, the Dodgers.

In time for opening day April 4, 2016, a huge new scoreboard was installed—59 feet high and 221 feet wide—giving 13,000 square feet of high definition formats. Also as part of renovation plans, new stat boards and a state-of-the-art sound system have also been installed. They also made Progressive Field Wi-Fi friendly for fans.

Life at Progressive Field has got tastier in recent years. Partnering with about a dozen local restaurants for stands within the stadium, the Indians kept that gastronomic expansion going into the 2017 season. Among the latest eating additions are varieties of pierogies, grilled Asian salmon, and veal parmesan sliders.

It has been announced the Indians and Progressive will host the Major League All-Star game in 2019.

Right: Players line the baselines as a brass band prepares to play the national anthem before a game between the Kansas City Royals and the Cleveland Indians. The Indians won the AL Central pennant seven times out of their first eight seasons in their new home of Jacobs Field.
Tom Pidgeon/Getty Images

Left: An August 2010 view of Progressive Field, Cleveland. After selling out its first 455 games, 1995–2001, by 2011 a jaundiced public was staying away. On April 3, 2011, only 8,726 turned up to watch the game. The 2015 annual attendance figure was a paltry 1,388,905, the lowest since 1992 at the old ballpark and a far cry from the 3,468,456 of 1999.
Beraxe via WikiCommons

Above: Aerial of downtown Cleveland on October 3, 1999. Jacobs Field can be seen in the foreground with what was then known as the Gund Arena above it. The new Cleveland Browns Stadium is to the upper right in the photo. This marked the first time both stadiums were used simultaneously: 43,012 were in attendance at Jacobs Field for the Cleveland Indians vs. Toronto Blue Jays game while 72,368 watched the Cleveland Browns play the New England Patriots
Paul M. Walsh via WikiCommons (CC BY 2.0)

Above Right: The view from the right-field seats during an Indians–Angels game. The distortion is due to the use of a fisheye lens.
Jeremy Burgin via WikiCommons (CC BY 2.0)

Right: View from above the visitor dugout with the Quicken Loans Arena—until 2005 the Gund Arena—and the Terminal Tower in the background. Terminal Tower was the fourth-tallest building in the world at its dedication on June 28, 1930.
Videojolt via WikiCommons (CC0 1.0)

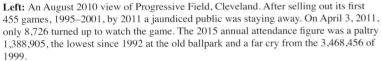

Right: Officially christened Lakefront Stadium when it opened in 1932, but more popularly known among fans of the resident Cleveland Indians as the "Mistake by the Lake," Municipal Stadium was used by the Indians until 1993.
National Baseball Hall of Fame

Far Right: After the last baseball game played in Cleveland Municipal Stadium in October 1993, it continued in service as the home of the NFL Browns until it was demolished in 1996 following the Browns' departure for Baltimore. Now a new "Cleveland Browns" team plays in Cleveland Browns Stadium built in 1997 on the site of the original Municipal Stadium.
National Baseball Hall of Fame

DETROIT TIGERS

COMERICA PARK

Address:
2100 Woodward Ave.
Detroit, MI 48201
Capacity: 41,299
Opening day: April 11, 2000—Detroit Tigers 5, Seattle Mariners 2
Cost to construct: $300 million
Architect: HOK Sports
Dimensions (ft):
Left Field—345
Left Center—370
Center Field—420
Right Center—365
Right Field—330
Defining feature: Scoreboard tigers
Little-known ground rule: Ball passing through or under the bullpen fence: two bases
World Series: 2006, 2012
All-Star Game: 2005
Memorable moments:

2000 April 11—Fans endure 34-degree temperatures to watch the Tigers beat Seattle in the park's first game.

2000 October 1—Shane Halter plays all nine positions on the final game of the season, the fourth major leaguer to do so.

2006 October 7—The Tigers beat the Yankees to take the divisional title 3–1.

2006 October 14—The Tigers sweep the Oakland As to reach the World Series but lose to the Cardinals.

2011 October 13—The Tigers win the fifth game of the ACLS to peg back the Rangers to 3–2, but go on to lose the next, and the series.

2012 October 28—The Tigers lose another World Series as Giants win 4–3 in the tenth to go 4–0.

2014 July—The Tigers became the first MLB team to have three consecutive Cy Young Award winners in their starting rotation: Justin Verlander, Max Scherzer, and David Price.

It is ironic that Detroit's baseball team moved from a place called Tiger Stadium. It is at Comerica Park that tigers roam.

Large tiger statues greet visitors outside. The perimeter is lined with tigers holding baseballs (actually lights) in their mouths. Two enormous tigers are positioned at either side of the scoreboard. They roar when the home team hits a home run. A merry-go-round featuring 30 hand-painted tigers entertains children along the first base side. There are even tiger claw marks scratched into concrete pillars around the park.

Comerica Park is a far cry from the no-nonsense, old-fashioned ambiance of Tiger Stadium, which sat on the well-worn intersection of Michigan and Trumbull, a corner where baseball was played for more than a century. Comerica Park's Ferris wheel (carriages are shaped like baseballs), its multi-colored water fountain that shoots "liquid fireworks," the air-conditioned bar, enormous state-of-the-art scoreboard, and the lack of a single pillar to block the view, would have been unthinkable at Tiger Stadium.

Oversized sculptures cast in stainless steel along the center field wall show six Tiger greats: Ty Cobb sliding spikes up, Willie Horton swinging, Al Kaline making a one-arm grab, along with Charlie Gehringer, Hank Greenberg and Hal Newhouser. Kaline's glove is positioned so that some day, some shot to deep center might just get caught.

The park's brick and steel construction and asymmetric dimensions mimic old parks, as does the dirt patch from the pitchers mound to home plate, a staple of turn-of-the-century fields. Originally the center-field flagpole was in play, just like at Tiger Stadium, though the fences were moved in and the flagpole now sits beyond the fence.

The Tigers' earlier stadium—the famous Tiger Stadium—was one of the famous "Jewel Box" stadiums from before World War 1, built as Navin Field. Renamed Briggs Stadium in 1934 and Tiger Stadium in 1961, the ballpark witnessed six World Series appearances and titles in 1935, 1945, 1968, and 1984. Over 20 years later, Comerica Park saw the Tigers win their first AL pennant but lose to the Cardinals in the World Series—as they had done in 1934 and 1968.

Since construction few major changes have been made: the most significant was in 2003, when the distance from left-center field to home plate was reduced from 395 to 370 feet. In 2005 this new space was utilized when the bullpens in right field were moved behind the left field fence and 950 seats added. Tiger Stadium had been hitter friendly; Comerica as built less so. The left field boundary alteration didn't change Comerica Park overnight, but batters were grateful.

Over last few years the GM Fountain became the Chevrolet Fountain; 2012 saw renovation and upgrading of the left-field video display; and in 2014 a $4 million renovation to the Pepsi Porch was announced.

On the field, the Tigers had a brilliant 2011 and 2012, winning back-to-back divisional titles, but losing out on the major prize, being beaten 4–2 by the Rangers in the ACLS; then losing the World Series to the Giants 4–0.

Long-time beloved Detroit sports team owner, philanthropist and entrepreneur Mike Ilitch died in February of 2017 at 87. The Tigers' team owner's name was etched into the grass in center field at Comerica Park in huge letters in time for opening day. The tribute reads "Mr. I."

A massive new $10 million center-right field videoboard made its debut at Comerica in 2017 and more out-of-town scores are now shown on scoreboards. Also, two new automobiles have been hung at the Chevrolet Fountain, replacing those that performed the duty for the 2016 season.

April 30, 2017 was Jewish Heritage Day at the park and Tiger great Hank Greenberg (1911–1986), the game's most prominent Jewish player of his era, was honored. As part of special ticket packages Tigers yarmulkes and a Greenberg Hall of Fame replica plaques were included.

Right: The Comerica Park Tigers at Gate B by Michael Keropian. Unsurprisingly, there are Tigers everywhere: the eyes of those on the scoreboard light up when a home run is hit.
Richard Cummins/Corbis

Above: A panorama of Comerica Park on June 4, 2006, showing the Red Sox playing the Tigers. Note the Detroit Lions' Ford Field peeping over the left-field grandstand.
Jake Novak via WikiCommons (CC BY 2.5)

This photo: It's fair to say that the Tigers' first years at Comerica Field produced few legendary performances. Reaching the World Series in 2006 saw an increase in fan numbers and four straight playoffs 2011–2014—including another World Series loss in 2012—ensured that annual attendance has hovered around the 2.75–3 million since 2006.
National Baseball Hall of Fame

Right: Unsurprisingly after 87 years in Tiger Stadium, many fans found the new ballpark less atmospheric than its predecessor. The general deterioration of parts of Detroit is also cited as reason to keep away. However, most open-minded reviews say the same thing: this is a good-looking, quirky ballpark with great sightlines and a great views.
Mark Hertzberg/National Baseball Hall of Fame

TIGER STADIUM (1912–99)
Home of the Detroit Tigers

Tiger Stadium smelled like old-time baseball. The game was first played at the corner of Michigan and Trumbull, a healthy stroll from downtown, in 1896. Tiger Stadium, originally Navin Field, was opened in 1912, the same week the Titanic sank, and the same day that Fenway Park opened in Boston. By 1938, the stadium had been fully enclosed, able to capture the fragrance of hot dogs, peanuts, and Cracker Jack for thousands of games to come. The second deck provided some of the best seats in baseball, and produced dramatic home runs that would disappear into the upper stands. A 125-foot high, center field flagpole sat in fair territory along the center field fence until the 1930s.

Tiger Stadium remained a fixture through the careers of Ty Cobb, Charlie Gehringer, Hank Greenberg, Al Kaline, and Willie Horton. It was here, on May 2, 1939, that the Yankees Lou Gehrig asked to be removed from the lineup, ending his iron man streak at 2,130 games.

With its obstructed views and rusted pillars, Tiger Stadium was in need of major repair by the 1990s, when the Tigers considered enclosing it with a dome and finally decided that a new facility was needed. Today the stadium remains standing as city planners try to figure out what else belongs at the famed Detroit corner.

Right: c. 1937 aerial view of Tiger Stadium. The upper deck was constructed over the outfield bleachers in this year; and the 125-foot flagpole in center field was removed at the end of the season.
National Baseball Hall of Fame

Michigan & Trumbull
Sept. 27, 1999
Detroit vs. Kansas City

Left: Tiger Stadium as seen on the occasion of the last game—Kansas City versus Detroit on September 27, 1999.
National Baseball Hall of Fame

KANSAS CITY ROYALS

KAUFFMAN STADIUM

Aka: Royals Stadium 1973–93
Address:
1 Royal Way
Kansas City, MO 64141
Capacity: 37,903
Opening day: April 10, 1973—Kansas City Royals 12, Texas Rangers 1
Cost to construct: $70 million
Architect: HNTB and Charles Deaton Design Associates
Dimensions (ft):
Left Field—330
Left Center—387
Center Field—410
Right Center—387
Right Field—330
Defining feature: Outfield waterworks
World Series: 1980, 1985, 2015
All-Star Game: 1973, 2012
Memorable moments:
1977 May 14—Jim Colborn pitches Royal's first no-hitter at the stadium, beating Texas 6–0.
1980 August 17—George Brett's goes four-for-four and raises his batting average to .400
1985 October 27—Royals win their first World Series on Bret Saberhagen's game seven shutout.
1986 September 14—Bo Jackson hits his first major-league home run, a 475-foot blast believed to be the longest in stadium history.
1991 August 26—Bret Saberhagen no-hits the White Sox.
2013 September 22—The Royals win their 82nd game of the season, to ensure only their second winning season since 1994.
2014 October 28—The Royals blow the Giants away 10–0 to take the World Series to a seventh game ... which they lose 3–2.
2015 October 28—The Royals win game two of the World Series and make no mistake at Citi Field.

If baseball stadiums are urban cathedrals, then Kauffman stadium is a rogue church.

There is no Waveland Avenue or Lansdowne Street hugging the fence at Kauffman Stadium, just freeway and farmland. Approaching from the West, one could drive hundreds of miles without seeing lights as bright as the standards atop the stadium, which draw insects from acres around.

Yet it is orthodox baseball they worship inside, as devout as anywhere else. At a time when other cities were building multi-sports complexes, the Royals was the only franchise to build a baseball-only stadium during the 1960s, 1970s, and 1980s. The site lines and seats all point toward the action. Grass replaced artificial turf in 1995, the fences were moved in, and the walls lowered.

Known for most of its life as Royals Stadium, it was renamed in honor of Ewing M. Kauffman who purchased the expansion team for Kansas City in 1968. If you want to date a color photo of Kauffman Stadium look at the seats. By the end of 2000, all of the red seats had been replaced by new blue ones.

If there is any monument to the era in which it was built, it is the 12-story high scoreboard, containing 16,320 lights, with a huge Royals crown on top, a Midwest version of Anaheim's Big A. The park's signature feature is a 322-foot wide water fountain spectacular—the largest privately funded waterworks in the world—which occupies the space that bleachers normally would. Major work was carried out during 2007–2009 largely to improve and expand the fans' amenities and facilities. This work led to, among other improvements, a state-of-the-art high definition scoreboard, wider concourses, new press facilities, new and better concessions, and improved facilities for children.

The improvements to the stadium ensured that in 2015 the Royals extended their lease to 2030. In 2012 they unveiled 120 solar panels the largest in-stadium solar array in MLB to provide around 36,000kWhr of renewable energy annually. Since 2014 they place a "W" on the Hall of Fame wall for every home win.

Two seasons after capturing the World Series, the Kansas City Royals showed off a spruced-up Kauffman Stadium to start the 2017 season. New amenities included renovation of the team store, making it more spacious, and technology on the main videoboard was upgraded, resulting in better picture clarity.

Also in 2017 a special exhibit was added to the team Hall of Fame because of the death of pitcher Yordano Ventura in an automobile accident. Royals players wore patches to honor the player in 2017 and a large photograph of the patch was displayed on a sign in the park.

Above: The stadium before the Indians played the Royals on Saturday May 6, 2017.
Nick Tre. Smith/Icon Sportswire via Getty Images

Right: All for a good cause! Some of baseball's premier power hitters stepped to the plate to support State Farm and MLB's effort to go to bat for charity. They raised $615,000 during the 2012 State Farm Home Run Derby.
State Farm via WikiCommons

Left: The old old matrix board and videoboard were installed in 1989. They have been replaced as can be seen in main photo.
Getty Images

Below Left: The Harry S. Truman Sports Complex—the Royals Stadium (lower) and Arrowhead Stadium, home of the NFL Kansas City Chiefs—in 1973 during that year's All-Star Game.
National Baseball Hall of Fame

This photo: Kauffman Stadium on August 10, 2014. The distinctive building on the hillside beyond the left field foul pole is the Fellowship of Christian Athletes. Note the scoreboard, ready for Opening Day 2008 when it was the largest HD LED display in the world. To the right of the scoreboard is the largest privately funded fountain in the world.
Mr.Konerko via WikiCommons (CC BY-SA 4.0)

MINNESOTA TWINS

TARGET FIELD

Address:
3rd Avenue N
Minneapolis, MN 55415
Capacity: 38,504
Opening day: April 12, 2010—Boston Red Sox 2, Minnesota Twins 5
Cost to construct: $390 million
Architect: Populous
Dimensions (ft):
Left Field—330
Left Center—387
Center Field—410
Right Center—387
Right Field—330
Defining feature: Gates named after retired numbers—center field gate #3 (Harmon Killebrew); left field gate #6 (Tony Oliva); home plate gate #14 (Kent Hrbek); right field gate #29 (Rod Carew); plaza gate #34 (Kirby Puckett)
World Series: None at Target Field; 1987, 1991 at the Metrodome
All-Star Game: 2014
Memorable moments:
2010 March 27—First game at the ballpark, a college baseball game between the University of Minnesota and Louisiana Tech.
2010 April 12—Jason Kubel hits the first home run at Target Field off Red Sox pitcher Scott Atchison.
2010 May 8—First doubleheader at Target Field, against the Orioles.
2010 October 6—The Twins play the first postseason game at Target Field, having won the Central Division championship. They lose to the Yankees.
2014 July—Hosted the 85th MLB All-Star Game and the Home Run Derby.

Few stadiums in baseball were more maligned than downtown Minneapolis' dome, regarded as among the worst venues in baseball. The Hubert H. Humphrey Metrodome, named after the former mayor, senator, and vice president, is no more, its Teflon-coated fiberglass ceiling no longer rising almost 20 stories in the air. It was demolished in 2014. The roof came into play on numerous occasions. In 1992, Chili Davis hit a towering drive which bounced off a speaker dangling from the roof. Rather than being a home run, it ricocheted into the glove of Baltimore second baseman Mark McLemore for an out.

Talk of a new stadium brewed in the Twin Cities for years. In the midst of playing some of their best baseball, but dogged by weak attendance and financial problems, the Twins were targeted in 2001–2002 by MLB for elimination (along with the Montreal Expos). The players union fought to stop the action, and the Twins were saved for the time being. The team continued its winning ways during and after the crisis, and its ownership stepped up efforts to get a new stadium.

In 2005, the Twins and Hennepin County came to an agreement for building a 42,000-seat, open-air, downtown ballpark. This location has certainly added to Target Field's popularity. There are plenty of bars, restaurants, and clubs nearby, but the trouble with a downtown historic warehouse area is size—or, rather, the lack it: eight acres bounded by, as the architects put it, "a complex labyrinth of city elements that formed the physical limitations of the site."

The ballpark was designed by Populous, the architects of Oriole Park at Camden Yards and PNC Park among others. Built at a cost of over $500 million, named after the Target Corporation in a deal announced on September 15, 2008, Target Field has no roof (both partners baulked at the extra $115 million cost) and so the Twins can enjoy the Minnesota elements, playing outdoors on grass for the first time in 28 years.

The stadium is equipped with a full roof-canopy soffit projecting out over the seating as well as "warming shelters" should the elements prove too much for the audience. Other facilities include the fourth largest scoreboard in MLB.

Since moving to the new stadium the Twins have had a torrid time. After reaching the playoffs six times in ten years up to 2010, since then there has only been one winning year as the team ended up fourth or fifth in the AL Central four years running. However, the franchise supports one of the best farm systems in the majors and there are signs that things may be improving.

Attendances, however, continue to suffer with the three million in 2010 becoming 2.2 million by 2015. During that time, it is true, the actual number of stadium seats has

been reduced from 39,504 to 38,871, but well-reviewed Target Field could do with the warmth a full house generates.

The shine has not worn off Target Field, so the main area for new development comes in the concession world, where some outlets offer seriously challenging meal combinations!

Above: The famous Minnie and Paul logo above the batter's eye animates at various points during a game—homers, when a Twin crosses home plate, for a strikeout, and for a Twins victory. The Mississippi seems to flow, the pair shake hands, and lights flash. *shiladsen via WikiCommons (CC BY 2.0)*

Right: An overview of Target Field before the game on April 3, 2010. *Lena Scherfenberg*

Left: Target Field night panorama. Opposite the photographer is the famous "Shaking Hands" logo that lights up when there's a Twins home run (see detail on page 86). Designed in 1961 by Ray Barton—who received the princely sum of $15 for the work—the logo has appeared on most of the Twins' uniforms ever since. *Jonathan Miske via WikiCommons (CC BY-SA 2.0)*

Above: 2010 panorama of Target Field.
Robaato via WikiCommons

Right: Target Field Armed Services Appreciation Day, July 3, 2011.
JL1Row via WikiCommons (CC BY-SA 3.0)

Opposite: Exterior view of the much maligned Metrodome.
Joseph Sohm; ChromoSohm Inc./Corbis

HUBERT H. HUMPHREY METRODOME (1982–2009)
Home of the Minnesota Twins

The Metrodome was loud, indoors, poorly carpeted, a hard place to spot balls, and a far, far cry from a field of dreams. It was here that the underrated Twins won the World Series in 1987 and 1991 without winning a single game in a National League park. It was here that Kirby Puckett and Torii Hunter turned a flexible baggy-like wall into a tool of defensive beauty. It was here that the descendants of Harmon Killebrew and Tony Oliva played baseball for six (and sometimes seven) months a year in a climate better suited for hockey. Few fields were more loaded with home-field advantages. The white Teflon roof made it difficult to pick up high-fly balls, particularly during day games. The screams of the homer hanky-waving fans in the 1987 World Series were measured by *Sporting News* at 118 decibels, about the same as a jet airplane on take-off. The odd curvature behind home plates made wild pitches routinely rebound toward first base. The Twins used it to their advantage. In their first World Championship season in 1987, the Twins were 56–25 in the Metrodome during the regular season, and 29–52 on the road. They went on to win the World Series by winning every game at home, a feat they would repeat four years later, prompting many opposing fans to call for the dome's destruction. The got their wish in 2014, when demolition took place in stages as its replacement, U.S. Bank Stadium, was built The Twins had left for the new, roofless Target Field for the 2010 season. The Metrodome became the home of the Vikings from 1982 to 2013, and it is the NFL team that will make U.S. Bank Stadium its home.

GRIFFITH STADIUM
(1911–61)
Home of the Washington Senators

"First in war, first in peace, and last in the American League," was the standing joke about the Washington Senators who spent half a century toiling in a ballpark so large that in four separate seasons the team could muster just a single home run in their home park.

It was at Griffith Stadium, about two-and-a-half miles from the White House, where William Taft became the first president to throw out a ceremonial first pitch, a ritual that was repeated by presidents through John Fitzgerald Kennedy. The centerfield indent, which made room for five duplexes that could not be razed, along with a large tree beyond the fence, gave the park a distinct character. The left field foul line, which at one point was 405 feet from home plate, made it a friendly park for pitchers, like Hall of Famer Walter Johnson, who called it home. Though the Senators had only fleeting moments of glory, it was also home to the successful Homestead Grays of the Negro League, and to Josh Gibson, who may have been professional baseball's finest power hitter.

After the 1960 season, the team moved to Minnesota and became the Twins. A new Senators team began playing at Griffith Stadium the very next year, but a desire for a more modern home prompted a move to Capitol Hill's RFK stadium. Griffith Stadium was knocked down in 1965.

Left: Just two-and-a-half miles from the White House, Griffith Stadium was the home of the Washington Senators for 50 years. For the 1961 season, the team moved to Minnesota and became the Twins. A new Senators team played at Griffith for a short time before moving to the newly built RFK Stadium. One of the distinctive features of Griffith was a 30-foot high wall that extended most of the length of right field, similar to the famous "Green Monster" at Boston's Fenway Park.
Martin Luther King, Jr. Library/National Baseball Hall of Fame

METROPOLITAN STADIUM (1961–81)
Home of the Minnesota Twins

Left: The Met was the ultimate suburban stadium, built on developing farmland, where parking was plentiful and far from bustling downtown. Its hodgepodge of grandstands and bleachers, surrounding a perfectly symmetrical field, was the result of a quick transformation from a minor league to a major league park, speeded up to lure the Twins from Washington. The grounds crew had a reputation for tailoring the infield to suit their team, which hosted a World Series in 1965, the team's fifth year in the Twin Cities. Minnesota's northern climate made outdoor games a challenge in April and September, let alone October, and by the early 1980s the Twins were playing downtown under a dome. The Mall of America now thrives on the site where the Met once stood.

AMERICAN LEAGUE WEST

The teams of the American League West are relatively young and so are their stadiums. The Athletics, who originally played in Philadelphia in the early 1900s, before moving to Kansas City in the 1950s, and eventually to Oakland, are the only exception. The LA Angels of Anaheim (originally the Los Angeles Angels, then the California Angels) came to life in the 1960s, as did the Texas Rangers (from Washington), and the Seattle Mariners were born in 1977. The latest addition to the league, the Houston Astros, arrived for the 2013 season, their retractable-roofed Minute Maid Park having opened in 2000.

The Texas Rangers and the Seattle Mariners moved into new stadiums in the 1990s to rave reviews from their fans, who in the teams' original homes had been subjected to Arlington's blistering heat and Seattle's impersonal dome. Anaheim has been quite comfortable in its home down the road from Disneyland since 1966, although now aged 50 the facility is becoming "The Big Aged." And Oakland A's fans enjoyed their oversized coliseum until the NFL Raiders returned in 1998, turning a baseball-friendly stadium into a football arena uncomfortably forced to hold 82 baseball games a year.

The A's would like to build a park of their own—Cisco Field in Fremont was one idea—and have applied to do so. They'd like to be somewhere else; trouble is, no one can decide where. Currently the Howard Terminal waterfront development looks like the front runner, but that could change overnight. In 2014, much to the Raiders' dismay, the A's signed a ten-year extension to their lease so until a new site is approved, the O.co Coliseum will continue to be their home.

Right: Globe Life Park in Arlington, the home field of the Texas Rangers.
The Lyda Hill Texas Collection of Photographs in Carol M. Highsmith's America Project, Library of Congress, Prints and Photographs Division

HOUSTON ASTROS

MINUTE MAID PARK

Aka: The Ballpark at Union Station (2000), Enron Field 2000-2002, Astros Field (Feb–July 2002)
Address:
501 Crawford Street
Houston, TX 77002
Capacity: 41,676
Opening day: April 7, 2000—Philadelphia Phillies 4, Houston Astros 1
Cost to construct: $248 million
Architect: HOK Sports
Dimensions (ft):
Left Field—315
Left Center—362
Center Field—436
Right Center—373
Right Field—326
Defining feature: Centerfield hill
World Series: 2005
All-Star Game: 2004
Memorable moments:
2001 October 4—Barry Bonds ties Mark McGwire's single season home run record, hitting No. 70 into the second deck.
2005 October 16—Astros take a 3–1 lead in the NLCS over the Cardinals. They go on to win 4–2.
2005 October 25—first World Series game to be played in Texas is also the longest World Series game ever played, lasting 14 innings and 5 hours and 41 minutes. Astros lose 7–5.
2005 October 26—Astros lose a one-run game and the World Series to the White Sox 4–0.
2010 April 5—Opening Day sees highest attendance total ever, with 43,836 tickets sold.
2013 March 31—The Astros win their first game in the American League's West Division.
2015 October 6—The Astros get the final play-off spot for the Wild Card game against the Yankees: they win 3–0 in NYC but lose to the Royals in the American League Division Series.

To appreciate the Astros' new home, think of the Houston Astrodome. Minute Maid Park is the opposite.

The Astrodome was a dark, completely enclosed, oversized gymnasium where power hitters went to die. Minute Maid Field is light, open, thoroughly unique, and conducive to scoring runs. Even when the retractable roof is closed, 50,000 square feet of glass panels allow patrons to gaze upon the Houston skyline or tropical storms passing above. In its time, the Astrodome represented an amazing architectural achievement, allowing Houston fans to watch their team despite the swampy heat and mosquitoes of summer. Over time, it came to represent everything that modern baseball parks try to avoid.

Now, the Astros play in a state-of-the art structure where the roof alone cost about twice what it took to build the Astrodome. Its most unusual quirk, Tal's Hill—named after team president Tal Smith—is a grassy knoll in dead center field, that rises at a 20 degree angle to a height of about five feet, prompting the most graceful centerfielders to watch their feet as they chase down deep fly balls. The Hill was Smith's suggestion when owner Drayton Lane asked what could be done to make the park different. Smith borrowed the idea for the hill from old Crosley Field in Cincinnati. On the left side of the incline used to be a flagpole, which was in play as at the old Tiger Stadium.

The left field bleachers are close, just 315 feet away, and protrude into the outfield, creating funny bounces and fantastic views. A one-of-a-kind porch hangs out over the outfield action, where walls come in several different shapes and heights. Small foul territories bring fans close to the field.

The park's signature feature is a 57-foot, 24-ton, 1860s steam locomotive, which chugs down an 800-foot track along the left field roof when the Astros do something special. Trains are a motif throughout the stadium. Most fans enter through the 1911 vintage Union Station, which forms the park's main entrance. The scoreboard is baseball's biggest, and explodes in celebration of every Astros' home run.

The park opened as Enron Field, after the Houston-based energy conglomerate which paid $100 million for 30 years of naming rights. Two years later, the energy conglomerate had gone bankrupt amid scandal. The large Enron sign remained on the park until the Astros bought back the naming right. Months later, they sold the rights to Minute Maid.

Minute Maid Park is a hitter-friendly ballpark, particularly in left field, which is just 315 feet away. Fielding is also made trickier in centerfield thanks to Tal's Hill, which is a piece of ground 90 feet wide with an incline of 30 degrees—just to make a fielder's job a little more difficult.

From 2013 the Astros started a new life with a change of ownership and a change of league, moving to the American League West. Unfortunately for the fans, this didn't improve the team's fortunes as they endured their third season with over a hundred losses.

In 2015 a $15 million renovation was announced that included removal of Tal's Hill in time for the 2016 season, but development was delayed for a further year when the Astros advanced to the playoffs.

Between the end of the 2016 season and the beginning of the 2017 season surgery was performed on the center field wall giving it a splashy new look. The wall is of differing heights at various spots, but on the field, the once-unique Tal's Hill was leveled so the approach run to the wall for fielders is flat. The deepest point in center was moved closer to home plate. The old spot of 436 feet is no more. Now the deep point is 409 feet.

There is now a flashy new mural highlighting some Astros' favorite players of the past. The changes have resulted in more seats being added in the deep part of the ballpark. This all came a year after the Astros installed LED lights at the park, a trend that is becoming more widespread in baseball.

Right: Opening Day, April 3, 2017, during the game between the Mariners and the Astros (the Astros won 3–0). The main difference between 2016 and 2017 is the disappearance of Tal's Hill and the shortening of center field to 409 feet. © *John Glaser*

Left: Aerial view of Enron Field and downtown Houston showing off the 242-foot high retractable roof. It takes between 12 and 20 minutes to open, and the roof moves back and forth an estimated 160 times a year.
Bob Daemmrich/Corbis

Opposite: Enron Field became Minute Maid Park for the 2003 season after an accounting scandal bankrupted the Houston-based energy conglomerate. This is an October 2012 view.
Daderot via WikiCommons (CC0 1.0)

Left: The sun goes down over Houston and Minute Maid Park on April 3, 2017. Note the 57-foot, 24-ton full-size replica steam loco that runs on an 800-foot track above left field. The park has a strong railway connection: the main entrance is the 1911 Union Station.
© *John Glaser*

ASTRODOME (1965–99)

The Houston Astrodome was hailed as the eighth wonder of the world when it opened, an architectural achievement that would change baseball's relationship to the elements. During the dome's 35-year baseball history, the Astros were rained out once, a enormous 1968 storm which didn't dampen the field, but prevented fans and the umpiring crew from making it to the park. Like a giant gymnasium, the Astrodome provoked awe in visitors who had never imagined indoor baseball, or an animated scoreboard with dancing figures for entertainment.

The Astrodome's field was originally grass, but the transparent roof created a menacing glare. The darkened panes killed the grass, and prompted the need for Astroturf, which become a standard for many other sports venues. Besides baseball, the Astrodome was host to musicians including the Rolling Stones, boxing matches, tennis tournaments, and the 1992 Republican National Convention.

Left: Aerial view of the Houston Astrodome, photographed in 2000.
Paul S. Howell/Getty Images

Right: The Houston Astrodome was the home of the Astros for 35 years 1965–2000.
National Baseball Hall of Fame

Left: A view of the Houston Astrodome during a game between the Chicago Cubs and the Houston Astros on August 29, 1996.
Getty Images

Right: Houston Astrodome on opening night, April 9, 1965, playing the Yankees in an exhibition game in front of President Lyndon B. Johnson.
National Baseball Hall of Fame

LOS ANGELES ANGELS OF ANAHEIM

ANGEL STADIUM OF ANAHEIM

Aka: Anaheim Stadium (1966–1997), Edison International Field of Anaheim (1998–2003)
Address:
2000 Gene Autry Way
Anaheim, CA 92806
Capacity: 45,050
Opening day: April 19, 1966—Chicago White Sox 3, California Angels 1
Cost to construct: $24 million
Architect: Robert A.M. Stern, HOK (renovations)
Dimensions (ft):
Left Field—347
Left Center—390
Center Field—396
Right Center—370
Right Field—350
Defining feature: The Big A
World Series: 2002
All-Star Game: 1967, 1989, 2010
Memorable moments:
1973 September 27—Nolan Ryan strikes out 16 Twins to establish a new record of 383 season strikeouts.
1986 October 12—Dave Henderson hits a two-out, two-run homer off Donnie Moore, to defeat the Angels who were within one strike of their first World Series appearance.
1990 September 14—Ken Griffey Jr. and Ken Griffey Sr. become first father-son pair to hit back-to-back home runs.
2002 October 27—Garret Anderson's bases loaded double in the third inning breaks a 1–1 tie and leads the Angels to a 4–1 win over the San Francisco Giants in game seven of the World Series.
2009 October 22—Yankee Nick Swisher pops out to end the fifth game of the ALCS to give the Angels hope. It's dashed in New York three days later.
2011—50th anniversary season. Players wear throwback jerseys for each Friday game.

Like much of Orange County, Angel Stadium was built on an old citrus grove, where oranges, alfalfa, and corn once grew. Anaheim in the 1960s was rapidly shedding its rural past. When Anaheim Stadium, as it was then known, opened in 1966, Disneyland had been open for just a decade, and nearby Los Angeles was spreading without restraint.

In that context, the preposterously enormous, 230-foot "A" reaching over the left-field wall to the sky, with a huge scoreboard and Standard Oil advertisement in the middle, and a golden halo on the top (that lights up when the Angels win), fit right in. Roughly modeled on Dodger Stadium, the state-of-the-art National League park where the Angels had spent the previous four seasons, the team's new home provided an identity for the "California Angels," owned by singing cowboy Gene Autrey.

The park had a distinct Southern California charm, palm trees, wide-open concourses, and immaculate concession stands, a far cry from the urban grit of eastern parks. The location was selected for its suburban ease, its ready freeway access and abundant parking.

The inside was made for baseball and nothing else. Short walls left outfielders to battle spectators for long fly balls. The triple deck contained no obstructed views. For its first two decades, the stadium had no bleachers at all, leaving the "Big A," and sometimes the distant San Gabriel mountains, looming as California icons.

The panoramic views ended after the 1979 season when the stadium was enclosed to add 20,000 seats for the NFL's Los Angeles Rams. The "Big A" was moved to the parking lot, where it remains today. In the 1990s, the Rams departed for St. Louis, the Disney Corp. assumed control of the Angels, and renovations were once again underway. This time $100 million was spent returning the park to its baseball-only status. The 20,000 football seats were replaced with bleachers, a state-of-the-art scoreboard, and the "California spectacular," an improbable backdrop of geysers shooting water 90 feet in the air, waterfalls flowing down a rocky mountainside, artificial rocks, and real trees—real Disneyland!

After nearly four decades of baseball in Anaheim, the Angels finally reached the World Series in 2002, winning in dramatic style against the Giants in game seven, at home.

In spite of its age the stadium continues to attract an average of over 40,000 fans to every game. Many of them would prefer a ground-up rebuild rather than a move to another location.

However, the stadium needs costly updating, and the Angels are contractually tied to staying until 2029, but have an opt-out until 2019. They lost out on acquiring nearby building land and are currently exploring other options for either major stadium upgrades or building an entire new ballpark in the region—although nobody seriously expects them to leave Anaheim.

The biggest recent ballpark change for the Angels is the installation of LED lighting, which makes things brighter. During the first games of the 2017 season Angel players said they took a little bit of getting used to!

Below Left: The Big A sign gives Angel Stadium its nickname. The halo lights up when the Angels win.
The Jon B. Lovelace Collection of California Photographs in Carol M. Highsmith's America Project, Library of Congress, Prints and Photographs Division

Below: Looking across the outfield to the unusual "California Spectacular" from where Angels' home runs and victories are feted by geysers and fireworks. Daktronics updated the scoreboards in 2004. At right, the main board has three electronic displays; the Prostar Display in the center is 42ft high by 67ft wide and alongside are two 11ft by 50ft displays. Opposite the camera is the Angel Vision Prostar video display, with two trivisions on each side. Atop the structure above the video board is an illuminated Angels "A."
Amin Eshaiker via WikiCommons

Left and Right: Originally Anaheim Stadium and later Edison International Field, Angel Stadium's entrance plaza is a relic of the period the franchise was owned by Disney. During that period, 1996–2003, the Angels won their first—and to date only—World Series; received a new (and much disliked) logo; and the ballpark renovations included the giant Angels' caps. They were blue; they were repainted red in 2002. Inside one of them is the size: 649.5.
The Jon B. Lovelace Collection of California Photographs in Carol M. Highsmith's America Project, Library of Congress, Prints and Photographs Division (Left); Kaizenmaster via WikiCommons (CC BY-SA 4.0)

Above: A view of Angel Stadium from the right field corner during the Angels' 6–3 win over the Dodgers on June 22, 2010.
Bspangenberg via WikiCommons (CC BY 3.0)

OAKLAND A'S

OAKLAND-ALAMEDA COLISEUM

Aka: Oakland-Alameda County Stadium (1968–97, 2008–11), Network Associates Coliseum (1998–2004), McAfee Coliseum (2004–2008), Overstock.co/O.co Coliseum (2011–2016)

Address:
UMAX Stadium, 1998
7000 Coliseum Way
Oakland, Ca. 94621

Capacity: 47,943 (for baseball)

Opening day: April 17, 1968 — Baltimore Orioles 4, Oakland Athletics 1

Cost to construct: $25.5 million

Architect: Skidmore, Owings & Merrill

Dimensions (ft):

Left Field—330

Left Center—388

Center Field—400

Right Center—388

Right Field—330

Defining feature: Mount Davis

World Series: 1972, 1973, 1974, 1988, 1989, 1990

All-Star Game: 1987

Memorable moments:

1972 September 22 — Gene Tenace hits two RBI to lead Oakland to a 3–2, World Series game seven victory over Cincinnati.

1979 April 17 — Just 653 fans show up to watch the A's beat the Mariners 6–5.

1988 October 18 — Mark McGwire's ninth-inning home run defeats Dodgers in World Series game three.

1989 October 14 — Dave Stewart dominates the Giants, and the A's take the first World Series game. Two weeks later they become world champions at Candlestick Park.

1990 October 20 — A big upset as Cincinnati take the fourth game of the World Series to win 4–0.

1991 May 1 — Rickey Henderson steals third base for his 939th stolen base, breaking Lou Brock's record.

It is not with affection that A's fans refer to the dreary slab of luxury boxes, clubs, and sky high grandstands which killed the bleachers, the ice plants, and the view of the East Bay hills, as "Mount Davis." While the rest of the country was making their ballparks better, Oakland was going in the opposite direction.

The Oakland-Alameda County Stadium, as it was known until 1998, had always been a workmanlike like place to see a baseball game. Huge foul territories annoyed batters and kept fans too far from the action. The symmetry reflected the era in which it was built. It looked less like a ballpark than a coliseum.

But except for the distances, there wasn't a bad seat in the house. The plain concrete confines were accessible, the bleachers relaxing, and the view of the Oakland hills, scarred by a huge quarry in dead center, let you know that you were in one of baseball's finest climates.

And then Al Davis brought the Raiders back to Oakland. The bleachers are now gone, the stadium is enclosed, and the new scoreboards are in perfect position only for a game with two end zones. The seats atop Mount Davis offer sweeping vistas of Mt. Tamalpais 20 miles in the distance, but no view of the warming track just below. Adding insult to the aesthetic change, the renovations weren't finished in time for the A's to begin their 1996 season, forcing them to open at a minor league park in Las Vegas. When fans were finally allowed back in (30 years to the day after then-Governor Ronald Reagan had thrown out the ceremonial first pitch at the stadium's inaugural game) they were given yellow construction hats with an A's logo.

The lack of collegiality between the football and baseball clubs is apparent on the A's Internet page, which refers dismissively to the coliseum as home to the Oakland Athletics and "Oakland's NFL franchise."

On the playing field, the wide foul territory is said to cost a batter five to seven batting average points over the course of a season, though it did not stop Reggie Jackson, Rickey Henderson, Jose Canseco, Mark McGwire, or Jason Giambi from hitting their stride. To the joy of most hitters, the fences have been moved in from their original locations, and the football enclosure keeps the wind down.

This was the home of Charlie Finley's innovations: orange baseballs, which were used in a 1973 exhibition game against the Indians, and gold-colored bases which adorned the infield for opening day 1970, a move the no-nonsense officials at Major League Baseball quickly banned. Besides the A's and Raiders, the coliseum was home to the USFL Oakland Invaders and has hosted scores of rock concerts from the Stones to Dylan.

Since losing the 1990 World Series, the best seasons have been two ALCS losses — in 1992 and 2006. Part of the problem, no doubt, is that for the last ten years the A's have expected a new ballpark but still have no idea where the team will be playing in the future. The concrete O.co Stadium is showing its age and the A's would like a dedicated stadium. But where do they move? The location the owners want (near San Jose in the lucrative heart of Silicon Valley) is within the territory of the Giants who are playing hardball. They don't want to give up the rights to that area to a rival MLB team who will start encroaching on their fan base. The proposal to move has spent five years gathering dust — so much so that San Jose has filed a lawsuit against MLB for the loss of earnings. But Oakland, too, wants to keep the team and a waterfront property is being promoted — this has MLB support but owner Lew Wolff has been implacably opposed. This confused situation will need resolving soon, meanwhile the A's are the only MLB team still sharing a stadium with an NFL team — and with no immediate change in sight.

By now one of the oldest stadiums in professional sports, Oakland Coliseum is likely to be replaced within a few years for the A's. As the Raiders plan to move to Las Vegas, leaving the Athletics as the only tenant, and the Golden State Warriors also plan to move to San Francisco, Oakland has warmed up to helping the A's build a new stadium to keep one big-league franchise in town. The Athletics are currently on a 10-year lease at Oakland-Alameda that runs through 2024 and the club agreed to look only within the city limits for

Above: Oakland-Alameda County Stadium taken in May 1994. The stadium changed its name in 1998 to the Network Associates Coliseum the first of a number of name changes that ended when a six-year naming rights deal—worth $1.2 million dollar—was signed with online retailer Overstock.com.
National Baseball Hall of Fame

Below: Fans sing "Take Me Out To The Ballgame" during the seventh-inning stretch at Oakland Coliseum 2000. San Francisco Chronicle

placement of a new stadium. Discussions heated up in the spring of 2017 for a new ballpark; in late April the team announced it has zeroed in on a location, but was not yet ready to publicly announce the site. A's management indicated it would like to see a neighborhood structure built, and with comparisons to the homey area surrounding the Chicago Cubs' Wrigley Field.

Far Left: The Coliseum is dual-use with both football and baseball played. This photo shows the Coliseum during an NFL game between the Oakland Raiders and the Baltimore Ravens on December 14, 2003. *Getty Images*

Inset: Satellite view of the stadium. *NASA via WikiCommons*

Left: The Coliseum before the start of a game between the Oakland Athletics and the Montreal Expos on June 15, 2003. The A's reached the playoffs every year between 2000 and 2003 and in 2006, ensuring attendances of around two million; a dip in fortunes saw a corresponding slide to 1.5 million until 2012. That year and in 2013 and 2014 playoff contention helped the crowds back up to two million a year—still nearly a million short of the figure of 2.9 million who watched in 1990 as the World Champion A's reached their third World Series in as many years. *Justin Sullivan/Getty Images*

SEATTLE MARINERS

SAFECO FIELD

Address:
First Ave. S and S. Atlantic St.
Seattle, WA 98104
Capacity: 47,116
Opening day: July 15, 1999—San Diego Padres 3,
Seattle Mariners 2
Cost to construct: $517 million
Architect: NBBJ
Dimensions (ft):
Left Field—331
Left Center—378
Center Field—401
Right Center—380
Right Field—326
Defining feature: Open-sided retractable roof
Little-known ground rule: If the roof is open and climatic
conditions warrant it, the roof can be closed in the
middle of an inning. Once the roof is closed during a
game, it will not be re-opened. If a game begins with the
roof closed, it may be opened only between innings and
the visiting team may challenge the decision to open it
World Series: None
All-Star Game: 2001
Memorable moments:
2000 September 30—Alex Rodriguez hits two home
    runs and bats in seven runs to beat the Angels and
    move Seattle into a first place tie.
2000 October 6—Carlos Guillen scores Rickey
    Henderson on a ninth-inning squeeze bunt to
    sweep White Sox in the division playoffs.
2001 July 11—Cal Ripken, in his final All-Star game, hits
    a third-inning home run and is named game MVP.
2001 October 6—Mariners win their 116th game, tying
    the Chicago Cubs major-league record.
2013—The Mariners hit the second most home runs in
    the AL (188) but fail to make the post season.
2016 June 2—The Mariners record their biggest-ever
    comeback in a 16–13 victory over the Padres,
    overcoming a fifth-inning 10-run deficit.

It took $517 million to move Seattle fans from baseball's worst stadium to one of its best, about the same dollar amount it took to construct every major-league park built in the United States through 1990—combined.

Real grass, cedar-lined dugouts, elevated bullpens, plus an old-fashioned, hand operated scoreboard and 11 video display boards. A concourse where fans waiting for salmon sandwiches, clam chowder, sushi rolls, or garlic fries won't miss the action.

There are 600,000 bricks in the facade, 40 miles of piping, 150 miles of electrical wiring, 200 miles of concrete, 535 metal halide lights, 600 tons of infield clay, and 20 to 30 miles of heating coils for the turf, which is a blend of Kentucky Bluegrass and perennial rye. And it wouldn't be Bill Gates' Seattle without Internet kiosks and luxury suites with high speed Internet access.

But what really cost money was the roof, which works like a well-vented convertible, (it has been compared to a "retractable umbrella") covering the stands and the field, but leaving the side open to allow fresh air to blow in. The 650-foot span retractable roof covers 10 acres and is stacked over the adjacent railroad tracks. When the roof is open, the right side of the upper deck offers views of downtown and the Puget Sound, though the city's landscape is not visible from most of the stadium.

The venue, though not the major leagues' coziest, are a vast improvement over the dark and cavernous Kingdome, the earlier home of the Mariners.

The park uniquely also features one more women's bathroom than men's, which may be a first at a sports venue.

The state-of-the-art park was built, owners said, to lure fans who in turn would bring in enough revenue to pay top-notch players to build a great team. Ironically, the stadium's astronomical cost put a serious dent in the owner's wallet, and now some of the Mariners' greatest, including Randy Johnson, Alex Rodriguez, and Ken Griffey Jr., have found homes elsewhere.

Thanks to the substantial investment in the facility, there have been no recent changes to the stadium, although 2013 saw the arrival of a new scoreboard—a monster, the biggest in the league at 11,000 sq ft—and the fences were moved closer to home plate.

However, the Mariners are replacing the system that opens and closes the roof at Safeco Field in an eight-phase job, hitting

the third phase in 2017. Back in 2015, the Mariners became the first team in the majors to install LED lighting in its ballpark. The improved lights reduce glare and shadows and are designed to last for 30 years. Other teams have followed the Mariners' lead.

Above: Safeco Field from Beacon Hill, December 13, 2011. It took the Mariners 14 years to record a winning season (in 1991) and the team has only reached the playoffs in 1995, 1997, 2000, and 2001.
Visitor7 via WikiCommons (CC BY-SA 3.0)

Right: Seattle is a fabulously beautiful city. Here the city's two main stadiums—the NFL Seahawks Stadium (closer to the camera) and Safeco Field, current home of the Seattle Mariners—are seen under white-topped mountains on June 25, 2003. Seahawks Stadium opened on July 19, 2002; Safeco on July 15, 1999.
Otto Greule Jr/Getty Images

Left: The Seattle Mariners play the Texas Rangers. The stadium is big and not very pretty, but has many good points that enable fans to have a very agreeable experience. The concessions are good with a lot of choice, the staff are friendly, and you can move about the stadium easily to maximise the range of views. Often full in the summer, attendance figures have improved in the last couple of years, so traffic can be a pain—but what's new? *Paul A. Souders/Corbis*

Left: Exterior view of Safeco Field on June 25, 2003.
Getty Images

This page: Safeco Field with roof retracted. Built to the south of the Mariners' old home, the Kingdome (see next page), the new stadium was named after Safeco, a financial services company whose roots in Seattle date back to 1923. Safeco will pay $1.8 million per year for the next 20 years.
Otto Greule Jr/Getty Images

Left: When it opened in 1977, the Kingdome was the American League's first indoor stadium. In 1994 four ceiling tiles fell before the start of a game causing the team to play its final 15 games on the road. Repairs cost $70 million. The stadium, then home to the NFL Seahawks as well as the Mariners, was spectacularly demolished in 2000. A new football-only stadium now occupies the site.
National Baseball Hall of Fame

Right: The dome itself was 660 feet in diameter and 250 feet from its apex to the playing surface. A batted ball hitting one of the speaker assemblies hung from the dome was considered to be in play. More than one hitter was "robbed" of a home run when a ball bouncing off a speaker was caught in flight for an out. Note the proximity to Puget Sound.
National Baseball Hall of Fame

TEXAS RANGERS

GLOBE LIFE PARK IN ARLINGTON

Aka: The Ballpark in Arlington (1994–2004), Ameriquest Field in Arlington (2004–06), Rangers Ballpark in Arlington (2007–13), The Ballpark at Arlington (2013–15)
Address:
1000 Ballpark Way
Arlington, TX 76011
Capacity: 48,114
Opening day: April 11, 1994—Milwaukee Brewers 4, Texas Rangers 3
Cost to construct: $191 million
Architect: HKS, Inc. and David M. Schwarz Architectural Services
Dimensions (ft):
Left Field—332
Left Center—390
Center Field—400
Right Center—381
Right Field—325
Defining feature: Center field office building
Little-known ground rule: Ball lodging in outfield fence padding or in the manually operated scoreboard in left field fence is a ground rule double
World Series: 2010, 2011
All-Star Game: 1995
Memorable moments:
1994 June 13—Jose Canseco hits three home runs and drives in eight runs in a 17–9 victory over Seattle.
1996 April 19—Juan Gonzelez, Dean Palmer, and Kevin Elster combine for 16 RBI as the Rangers beat O's 26–7.
1997 June 12—In baseball's first regular-season interleague game, San Francisco beats the Rangers 4–3.
2010 October 22—Victory over the Yankees in the sixth game of the ALCS wins the Rangers their first American League pennant.
2010 October 30—The Rangers win the first World Series game ever won by a team from Texas, beating the Giants 4–2.

Take a bit of Ebbets Field, some Tiger Stadium, a little Yankee Stadium, some Wrigley Field, and a touch of Camden Yards. Mix in a lot of Texas, put it in a suburban parking lot, and you approach the Globe Life Park at Arlington.

The asymmetrical outfield is like Ebbets Field, with eight facets sending hard-hit balls in different directions The double-decked, right-field porch is like Tiger Stadium, though it is too deep to catch as many home runs. The bleachers recall Wrigley. The canopy lining the upper deck is reminiscent of Yankee Stadium. The brick arches on the exterior feel like Camden Yards.

Yet this is Texas. Cast iron Lone Stars adorn aisles seats, replicating those on the building's facade. Large steer skulls and murals depicting the state's history decorate the walls, and a brick "Walk of Fame," celebrating Ranger's history surrounds the park. The grass in the batter's line of vision in dead center is named Greene's Hill after former Arlington Mayor Richard Greene. There is a Texas-sized dimension to the entire stadium complex, which includes a 12-acre, man-made lake (named for late Rangers broadcaster Mark Holtz), a 17,000 square-foot baseball museum said to be the largest outside Cooperstown, a 225-seat auditorium, a children's learning center, a four-story office building, and a kid-sized park with seats for 650 just outside.

To battle the Texas elements, the stadium is sunken, out of the wind, and enclosed by the office building, home to the Ranger's front office, just beyond center field. A giant windscreen, 42 feet high and 430 feet long, was installed on the roof to further reduce wind. Overhead fans in the upper and lower deck porches help keep patrons cool.

The $191 million park was paid for largely through a sales tax increase, pushed through by the team's managing partner in the early 1990s, George W. Bush.

With six postseason appearances, including two World Series, between 1996 and 2012, the Rangers have an excellent playing record in recent years. Their hitter-friendly ballpark has certainly helped, with eight 200+ home run years 1996–13, including the remarkable 260 in 2005. The Texas temperatures still lead to the question of why there is no roof, but renovations in 2010–2011, including new Daktronics displays, ensure that the ballpark is up to date.

In February 2014 the Globe Life and Accident Insurance Company—based in Dallas—bought the naming rights to the stadium.

At the moment the only action in improvements in fan life at Globe Life Park are going to be in the concessions world. This is because in the November 2016 elections, fans went to the polls and voted to fund a new stadium right next door to Globe Life with

the idea of it opening in time for the 2020 season—despite the fact that Globe Life was built as recently as 1994, when it was called The Ballpark in Arlington.

A key feature of the new stadium, (which this one lacks), is a retractable roof: it is expected to be a popular feature with fans during the intensely hot and humid Texas summers.

As part of the overall project, an entertainment center featuring sports bars, restaurants, and a hotel are scheduled to be built between the old park and the new one.

Right: The imposing entrance to what was then The Ballpark in Arlington and since February 2014 has been named Globe Life Park in Arlington.
Ronald Martinez/Getty Images

THE BALLPARK IN ARLINGTON

TICKETS

1998 view of the Ballpark in Arlington.
Joseph Sohm; Visions of America/Corbis

This 2016 panorama of Globe Life Park was taken standing behind Section 226. The Rangers took 25 years to reach the playoffs for the first time (in 1996). They reached their first World Series in 2010 losing 4–1 to the Giants. The next year it was closer: 4–3 to the Cardinals. In 2012 the Rangers recorded their first three-million season with 3,460,280 coming to see if they could make it three in a row. Sadly they didn't and in 2015 the gate was a million smaller at 2,491,875.
Dopefish via WikiCommons

Right: Texas-sized in every way, this is how the Ballpark at Arlington appeared when constructed. It boasted a 12-acre man-made lake, a baseball museum said to be the largest after the Hall of Fame in Cooperstown, and a four-story office building. *National Baseball Hall of Fame*

Left: To provide the players some protection from the harsh Texas winds, the playing field is sunken and surrounded by tall, wind-blocking structures and screens.
National Baseball Hall of Fame

The National League of Professional Baseball Clubs, now known simply as the National League, was formed in 1876, the year of Custer's last stand, and exactly 100 years after the United States declared its independence. Some of its eight charter cities are familiar baseball towns: Chicago, Cincinnati, Philadelphia, St. Louis, and Boston. Others were unable to hold their teams: Hartford, Brooklyn, and Louisville.

The National League now consists of 16 teams, which have been divided into three divisions since 1994. Its newest franchises are located in places like Arizona and Colorado, which weren't even part of the union when the league was founded.

Today, the National League is experiencing a stadium explosion. Only three teams play in stadiums built prior to 1993. Ten new National League parks have been opened since 2000, including Citizen's Bank Park in Philadelphia and Petco Park in San Diego, which opened their doors in 2004; the third Busch Stadium in 2006; the new Nationals Park in 2008; Citi Field in 2009; and the most recent, Marlins Park, in 2012.

Left: Panorama of Turner Field as the Atlanta Braves play a night game in April 1997.
Joseph Sohm; ChromoSohm Inc./Corbis

NATIONAL LEAGUE EAST

The National League East is a division that has seen massive changes in the last few years. The pre-turn-of-the-century teams, the Braves and the Phillies, play in brand-new, highly regarded ballparks. Of the others, the Mets have a new stadium, Citi Field; the newly arrived Nationals have purpose-built Nationals Park; and the Marlins moved into a new stadium in 2012.

Two stadiums in the National League East Division were built for Olympics. Another was built for football. Montreal's Le Stade Olympique was constructed for the 1976 Summer Olympics, and converted for the Expos the following year. The result was an oversized, clumsy park that never felt quite right for baseball. Little surprise that the franchise moved to Washington in 2005. Twenty years later, the Braves learned from the Expos' mistakes. Atlanta's stadium for the 1996 Summer Games was specially designed to transform into a baseball friendly park, although the Braves intend to leave it in 2017.

New York's Shea Stadium was built for baseball, though it was also enlisted for football, concerts, boxing matches, and religious events. It, too, was superseded by a new ballpark, which opened in 2009.

Miami's Marlins Park is the most recent of the ballparks in the National League East, located on the old Miami Orange Bowl site.

The Atlanta Braves hold the most divisional titles at 12, followed by the Philadelphia Phillies on 11. The current title holders, the New York Mets, have a long way to catch up with only six titles.

Shea Stadium at dusk during the National League game between the Philadelphia Phillies and the New York Mets on July 13, 2003.
Jerry Driendl/Getty Images

ATLANTA BRAVES

SUNTRUST PARK

Right: SunTrust Park Opening Day 2017.
Thechased at English Wikipedia (CC BY 4.0)

Address:
755 Battery Avenue
Atlanta, GA 30339
Capacity: 41,149
Opening day: April 14, 2017—Atlanta Braves 5, San Diego Padres 2
Cost to construct: $1.1 billion
Architect: Populous
Dimensions (ft):
Left Field—335
Left Center—385
Center Field—400
Right Center—375
Right Field—325
Defining feature: Beyond the center field wall SunTrust features three evergreen trees, a waterfall and boulder nature design. The fountain water gushes 50 feet into the air to a higher pond
World Series: None yet!
All Star Game: None yet!
Memorable moments:
2016 October 2—Last Braves regular season game at Turner Field.
2017 April 14—Right-hander Julio Teheran threw six innings and became the first pitcher and first Braves pitcher to win a game in the new SunTrust Park by beating San Diego, 5–2.
2017 April 14—Braves center fielder Ender Inciarte hit the first home run ever at SunTrust Park.

It was barely more than two decades ago when the Atlanta Braves introduced a new ballpark to their fans. Turner Field was carved out of the structure created for the opening ceremonies of the 1996 Summer Olympics, replacing Atlanta-Fulton County Stadium.

In 2017, Major League Baseball welcomed SunTrust Park to the exclusive membership of big-league ballparks as the new home of the Braves. After decades of playing baseball in downtown stadiums, the Braves now play in the Atlanta suburbs. The new park was built outside of downtown, 10 miles to the northeast, in Cobb County. The timing to strike out fresh with a new park, although Turner Field was not very old, was when the club's 20-year lease expired. Braves management also contended Turner Field was in need of $350 million in renovations to stay current. Team officials also stated Turner Field's maintenance costs were higher than at other ballparks because of its original needs for other purposes beyond baseball. Other problems cited as inconvenient for fans were limited parking and downtown traffic congestion.

SunTrust is a start-from-scratch park built at a cost of $1.1 billion with public-private financing. The Braves themselves will contribute $181 million a year for 10 years to help retire the bond debt.

Although the closest train station is 10 miles from the stadium, the Braves committed to a bus plan to help fans travel back and forth to the new park. The team also announced an expenditure of $400 million to establish an entertainment district around SunTrust—a concept that other teams have been exploring and investing in recently. The goal is to establish a street outside the stadium lined with restaurants, bars and shops.

Consistent with the prevailing notion of new ballparks containing high-grade fan amenities, yet retaining a more historical, retro look, the Braves hired the firm Populous, which had already designed 19 other Major League stadiums.

In an interesting twist, Eutis Morris, then 83, laid the first brick in the construction of the ballpark in August of 2015. Morris had also laid the first brick for the construction of Fulton County Stadium and the first and last brick at the Olympic Stadium. Also, at the beginning of construction, the team participated in the laying of two time capsules which included some Braves materials dating back as far as a 1948 World Series program from when the team was still playing in Boston.

As a trial run for play in 2017, the Braves first competed in an exhibition game against the New York Yankees on March 31. The University of Georgia played a Southeastern Conference game against the University of Missouri on April 8 and attracted more than 33,000 fans, many present to inspect the premises.

On the main concourse behind home plate is Monument Garden, which displays baseball-themed artwork, other team memorabilia, and a statue of all-time great Hank Aaron. Outside SunTrust Park are statues of Hall of Fame manager Bobby Cox, which was unveiled April 13, 2017, the day before the park's opening, 300-game winner Phil Niekro, and Warren Spahn, the left-handed pitcher with the most recorded wins in history.

As is often the case at ballparks in the modern era, much more thought was given to the food for sale beyond the basics of peanuts, Cracker Jack and hot dogs. A theme for the new SunTrust was southern cooking as the Braves wished to remain close to Atlanta's roots. These beyond-the-norm menu items were labeled "Taste of Braves Country." Among other items, one can also purchase a pretzel in the shape of the Braves' "A."

The official grand opening of SunTrust Park took place on April 14, 2017 when Atlanta defeated the San Diego Padres, 5–2. During a special ceremony the team showed off the club's 10 retired numbers in a display on the building façade in left field. In attendance were Braves luminaries Aaron, Cox, Tom Glavine, John Smoltz, Niekro, Chipper Jones, and Dale Murphy. The first five are enshrined in the Baseball Hall of Fame and Jones is expected to be elected soon after becoming eligible. Aaron, then 83, and one of the greatest hitters in baseball history, threw out the ceremonial first pitch. Cox, the retired manager, caught it.

Right: SunTrust Park—view from right field May 9, 2017. The move to Cobb County divided Braves' fans. Some thought the move from a perfectly acceptable, working stadium to a new out of town location just invited traffic problems? Why not spend money on a decent upgrade and improve the existing neighborhood. Others were delighted to have a new field purpose-built for baseball. Had the Ted been known for its winning ways, things might have been different, but it had a 15–22 postseason record and just one World Series (a loss). Fans' immediate reactions to the new ballpark have been *Thomson200/WikiCommons (CC0 1.0)*

Opposite:
Right: Javy Lopez—#8 of the Atlanta Braves—flies out to left fielder Miguel Cabrera of the Florida Marlins in the seventh inning of the game on July 23, 2003, at Turner Field.
Jamie Squire/Getty Images

Below: The National League Wildcard Game between the Atlanta Braves and the St. Louis Cardinals on October 5, 2012. Note the video display, at the time the world's largest, and two distinctive advertising fixturesbehind left field— a Coca-Cola bottle and the 40-foot-tall Chick-fil-A cow, added in 2008.
MKultra via WikiCommons

TURNER FIELD
(1997–2016)
Home of the Atlanta Braves

Turner Field was born an 85,000-seat, Olympic-sized track and field coliseum. The Olympics came to Atlanta in 1996, just as the Braves were itching for a new home after playing for three decades in oversized Atlanta-Fulton County Stadium. The Braves and the city struck a deal. The city built a $207 million Olympic stadium in the parking lot of the Braves' old home. When the Olympians went home, the Braves spent another $35 million to turn the mega-sports complex into a baseball-only facility. It took a close look to detect the stadium's Olympic lineage. One clue was the unusual outfield, where center and left field were curved, like stadiums built in the 1960s, a holdover from the oval-shaped Olympic Stadium, while the right-field fence was a straight line consistent with today's old-style parks. In November 2013 the Braves announced they would not be renewing the lease on the Ted (which expired in 2016) and would leave for a new ballpark. Georgia State University acquired the site and their redevelopment includes a new football stadium.

Main photo: Kenny Lofton—#7 of the Chicago Cubs—bats against the Atlanta Braves in the second inning of the National League Divisional Series Game 2 on October 1, 2003 at Turner Field. The Braves defeated the Cubs 5–3. The Braves are used to the playoffs: from 1991 to 2005 they won 14 consecutive divisional titles, reached the World Series five times and won in 1995 before moving to their new ballpark.
Craig Jones/Getty Images

Inset: A panorama of Turner Field made on July 17, 2012. *Sreejithk2000 via WikiCommons (CC BY-SA 3.0)*

ATLANTA-FULTON COUNTY STADIUM
(1966–1996)
Home of the Atlanta Braves

Built in less than a year, part of what lured the team from its home in Milwaukee, enclosed, symmetrical and modern, this ballpark was known as a place to hit home runs. The power of the park was enhanced by its elevation 1,000 feet above sea level, not as thin-aired as the mile high environs of Denver, but giving batters a few extra feet on long fly balls. The stadium's most famous home run came on opening day, April 8, 1974, when Hank Aaron hit No. 715 over the left field wall, sending him on a well-photographed, round-the-bases trot into baseball immortality. The stadium served admirably for 30 years, hosting four World Series in the 1990s, as the once-woeful Braves became the team of the decade. The stadium's final game was a 1–0 loss to the New York Yankees in the 1996 World Series.

Left: Construction began in 1964 on a structure that needed to be open in time to receive the Milwaukee Braves who were scheduled to move to Atlanta in time to play on Opening Day 1966. Astonishingly, construction was completed a year early. After Hank Aaron hit his 500th homerun there on July 14, 1968, the park was sometimes referred to as the "House that Hank Built," a not so subtle reference to another ballpark made famous by the balls that George Herman Ruth hit out of it.
National Baseball Hall of Fame

MIAMI MARLINS

MARLINS PARK

Address:
51 Marlins Way
Miami, Florida
Capacity: 36,742
Opening day: April 4, 2012—Florida Marlins 1, St Louis Cardinals 4
Cost to construct: $634 million
Architect: Populous
Dimensions (ft):
Left Field—344
Left Center—386
Center Field—407
Right Center—392
Right Field—335
Defining feature: That roof (or the Marlinator)
World Series: None
All-Star Game: 2017 (projected)
Memorable moments:
2012 April 12—First win at Marlins Park of the new season, 5–4 in the 11th against the Astros (a score line repeated on April 15).
2012 May 30—Victory over the Nats gives the Marlins a 21-win May, a franchise record. At 29–22 the season could go both ways ... unfortunately it's downwards and the Marlins ended the season at the bottom of the National League East.
2015 July 2—Jose Fernandez returns from surgery, earns a win, and blasts a homer as well. If he's fit next year ...

Pick up the park and move it 500 miles north, and you've got a real winner—wrote ESPN columnist Jeff Merron about the stadium the Marlins started with. And soon after the Marlins were created, the owners were already looking for ways to let them play under a retractable dome, either in downtown Miami, or at Pro Player.

The heat didn't stop the new franchise gaining immediate success. The Marlins won their first game on April 5, 1993: five years later they won their first World Series. Five years later, they won again, beating the Yankees in six games.

No matter the success, the Marlins needed a roof to protect fans and players from the regular rains and the high temperatures. It cost over $600 million to achieve the stadium controversial owner Jeffrey Loria wanted, but by 2012 there it was, risen like a phoenix from the ashes of the Miami Orange Bowl. Above the 37,000-capacity crowd (the team has moved from the largest stadium in baseball to the smallest) runs MLB's fifth retractable roof. It is formed from three metal-decked operable panels, the center panel at the highest elevation with 200 feet clear over second base to allow for "pop-flies." The 338,000 square feet of roof surface area—some 19 million pounds—can open or close within 13 minutes, traveling at a speed of 39 feet per minute. Average game temperatures have dropped from 85°F to 75°F.

As you look through the huge window towards downtown Miami, your eye is drawn to a bizarre, multicolored edifice behind the outfield fence in left-centerfield. After a Marlin homerun the colorful, $2.5 million, 75ft tall structure provides moving waves along the bottom and spins marlins, seagulls and flamingos.

Enormous effort has gone into making the entire facility as eco-friendly as possible and in May 2012 Marlins Park officially became the MLBs most sustainable ballpark. For the start of the 2016 season the park was renovated at a cost of $500,000; most of the expense was spent lowering and moving in the outfield walls, this also eliminated the "Bermuda Triangle" in center field.

Is the new stadium a bizarre misjudgment or a brilliant coup? The jury's still out.

The All-Star game headed to Miami for the first time in 2017, an event which put the hosts and Marlins Park in the national spotlight on July 11. It was with an eye towards this event that in 2016 the Marlins expanded the food offerings and added more stands around the ballpark. There are not many places around the big leagues (or anywhere else come to that) where a fan can buy Cuban ice cream specialties for dessert after a main course of a selection of various grilled cheese sandwiches.

Above and Right: The field at Marlins Park with the Miami skyline in the background. In left centerfield is the Marlinator (detail above) that animates should the Marlins hit a home run. The Marlins Park design also provides an open east end to provide unobstructed views to the downtown Miami skyline.
Dan Lundberg via WikiCommons (CC BY-SA 2.0)

Above: Marlins Park on May 16, 2015. The Marlins haven't started well at the new ballpark with five losing seasons, although the new stadium has lifted attendances.
WPPilot via WikiCommons (CC BY 4.0)

SUN LIFE STADIUM (1993–2011)
Home of the Florida Marlins

Built for football, it took some doing—and about $10 million—to make it compatible for baseball, the first football stadium to be so converted. A hydraulically operated pitcher's mound was installed, a new press box for baseball media was added, and baseball locker rooms built. Due to its football-sized dimensions, huge numbers of empty orange seats, trimmed in teal and blue, made for a colorful but empty appearance. The Marlins decided to close the upper deck with blue tarps, limiting capacity and lending the park a more intimate feel. The entrance to the park, surrounded by pastel colors and palm trees, was unmistakably Florida. So is the weather, which often makes it uncomfortably hot during day games and thunderstorming at night.

Originally built as the John Robbie Stadium in 1987, the facility enjoyed many other names—Pro Player Park (or Stadium) in 1996–2005, Dolphin (or Dolphins) Stadium 2005–2009, Land Shar Stadium 2009–2010, and finally from 2010, Sun Life Stadium.

From the start the stadium saw a remarkable amount of post-season excitement. In 1997, the Marlins stunned the baseball world by winning the World Series in seven games over the Cleveland Indians. Attendance suffered when the old owners sold off the team's best talent, but a new crop of Marlins repeated the triumph in 2003 with a surprise six-game World Series victory over the New York Yankees. The success led to a new stadium and Sun Life reverted to football full-time.

Above: A night exterior view of Pro Player Stadium. *Digitalballparks.com*

Above Right and Right: Two more views of Pro Player Stadium. Built by Wayne Huizenga after he had bought the Miami Dolphins, it cost $10 million to renovate the stadium for baseball. In 1996 Pro Player, a division of Fruit-of-the-Loom, bought the naming rights to the stadium. *Digitalballparks.com*

NEW YORK METS

CITI FIELD

Address:
Roosevelt Avenue, Flushing.
Queens, NY 11354
Capacity: 41,922
Opening day: April 13, 2009—San Diego Padres 6,
New York Mets 5
Cost to construct: $900 million
Architect: Populous
Dimensions (ft):
Left Field—335
Left Center—358
Center Field—408
Right Center—375
Right Field—330
Defining feature: Noisy jets flying in and out of La
Guardia. The Mets Magic Top Hat with its red apple
rising out when a Mets' player hits a homer.
World Series: 2015
All-Star Game: 2013
Memorable moments:
2009 March 29—First game played at Citi Field, a
college game between St. John's and Georgetown.
2009 April 13—Jody Gerut becomes the first player in
MLB history to open a ballpark with a home run.
2009 April 15—The Mets beat the Padres 7–2 for their
first win at Citi Field.
2009 April 17—Gary Sheffield hits his 500th home run
against the Milwaukee Brewers.
2009 July—Paul McCartney performs three sold-out
concerts at Citi Field.
2011 August 15—Against the Padres in a 5–4 win Jason
Isringhausen becomes the 23rd pitcher to record
300 career saves.
2012 June 1—Johan Setana records the first no-hitter in
Mets' history, against the Cardinals in an 8–0 win.
2015, April 23—Mets tie a franchise season record of 11
straight wins.
2015, October 30—The first Mets World Series game in
New York and first ever at Citi Field, ended with a
9-3 New York victory.

The Mets have been playing in the National League's Eastern Division since 1969. They entered the league as an expansion team in 1962 and played at the old Polo Grounds. Even though managed by the legendary Casey Stengel, the Mets were easily one of the worst teams in history. They made their swansong at the Polo Grounds on September 18, 1963, and transferred to the new Shea Stadium in 1964.

Few parks in baseball possessed so many memories and so little soul as Shea. Opened in an era of cookie-cutter parks, Shea's builders boasted of its symmetrical geometry, its grand four-story escalator system, its tall ramps, its tidy four-tier layout, and its lack of view-blocking pillars. It was the first stadium built able to make a rapid transition to football, and one of the first to feature a novel "color" scoreboard.

It was a wonder in a time gone by. Today, its most remarkable feature is its noise, which has nothing to do with its fans, but the stadium's unfortunate location in the flight path of New York La Guardia Airport, which averages more than 1,000 flights a day. The disrupting engine roar, which has prompted some players to wear earplugs, is a constant reminder that this is not a quaint ball yard. The stadium, originally to be called Flushing Meadows Park, was instead named after the lawyer who led the effort to bring the Mets to New York, returning National League baseball to New York after the departure of the Dodgers and the Giants in 1957.

William Alfred Shea christened the stadium with two bottles of water—one from the water near Ebbets Field, the Dodgers' old home, and one from the Harlem River near the Polo Grounds, where the Giants had played (and the Mets spent their first two seasons.)

As bad as the Mets were at the beginning, they turned things around in a big way in 1969. That year, the "Miracle Mets" came from far behind to catch the Cubs late in the season, knocked off the Braves in the playoffs, then stunned the favored Baltimore Orioles in the World Series 4–1. The team returned to baseball's championship in 1973, 1986, and 2000. In 1986 they defeated the Red Sox in seven games, but they lost crosstown series to the Yankees in 1973 and 2000.

They left Shea Stadium for the new Citi Field at the end of the 2008 season. Named after the Citigroup financial service company, it is only a few yards away from Shea, built on one of its parking lots. Citi Field has a retro feel to it. Designed by the then HOK Sport, the exterior is clad in traditional materials such as limestone, granite, cast stone, and brick—the latter's color a close match to that used at Brooklyn's old Ebbets Field. Arches add to the retro feel. The front entrance features a rotunda named after Brooklyn Dodgers legend Jackie Robinson. The field will make a fine home for the Mets for years to come.

Few home runs were hit in the early years and Citi Field became known as a "pitcher's park," so for the 2012 season the ballpark's dimensions were altered to create a more neutral ballpark: both players and fans were pleased with the improved results.

In an ethnically diverse city, the Mets keep adding ethnically diverse food choices to their concessions lineup, including in some instances going back to the basics. In 2017, a dish that was basically Mac and Cheese with a twist was added—it has roast brisket on top. Also included on the menu was catch-of-the-day seafood.

Right: Citi Field's irregular outfield dimensions, classical façade, and intimate seating bowl are reminiscent of baseball's old ballparks, while the high-tech scoreboards, comfortable seats, and ample amenities provide the ultimate in modern conveniences.
Rob Tringali/Sportschrome/Getty Images

Above: The granite, limestone, and brick exterior of Citi Field, along with the arched windows and gates are inspired by the design of Brooklyn's Ebbets Field and other classic ballparks of an earlier era.
Al Bello/Getty Images

Right: In an era of cookie-cutter parks, Shea Stadium was distinctive not for its architectural features, but for its location below the flight path of New York's La Guardia airport With an average of 1,000 a day, even the players sometimes wore earplugs.
National Baseball Hall of Fame

SHEA STADIUM
(1964–2009)
Home of the New York Mets

Built as a dual purpose facility—moveable stands allowed easy conversion for football—Shea is perhaps most famous to the outside world as being the place where Beatlemania hit the US, thanks to the August 15, 1965, concert. The Beatles opened their 1965 North American tour there to a record audience of 55,600. Shea was the scene of many concerts after that, audience levels reaching 70,000. It was a hugely successful ballpark, too, although proximity to LaGuardia Airport made it noisy. In 1969, the "Miracle Mets" came from far behind to stun the baseball world and, eventually in the World Series, the Baltimore Orioles. There would be three National League Division Series played at Shea (1999, 2000, and 2006), seven National League Championship Series (1969, 1973, 1986, 1988, 1999, 2000 and 2006) and three more World Series (1973, 1986, and 2000). In 1986 the Mets defeated the Red Sox in seven games, but they lost to Oakland in 1973 and the crosstown series to the Yankees in 2000.

Right: Shea Stadium from the upper deck during the game between the Philadelphia Phillies and the New York Mets on July 13, 2003. The Mets won 4–3. The stadium had been designed to be expanded. However, when plans were drawn up to add seats and cover the stadium with a dome, they had to be scrapped because the engineers said the stadium could collapse under the weight.
Jerry Driendl/Getty Images

Left: Shea Stadium at dusk during the July 13, 2003 game between the Phillies and the Mets.
Jerry Driendl/Getty Images

PHILADELPHIA PHILLIES

CITIZENS BANK PARK

Address: Pattison Avenue, Philadelphia
Capacity: 43,647
Opening Day: April 12, 2004. Cincinnati Reds 4, Philadelphia Phillies 1
Cost to construct: $346 million
Architect: Ewing Cole Cherry Brott (ECCB) and HOK
Dimensions (ft):
Left Field—329
Left Center—374
Center Field—401
Right Center—369
Right Field—330
Defining feature: Electronic Liberty Bell set off by home run
World Series: 2008, 2009
All-Star Game: None
Memorable moments:
2004 April 12—Bobby Abreu of the Phillies hit the ballpark's first home run.
2008 October 25—the Phillies defeat the Tampa Bay Rays, 5–4 in Game 3. of the World Series
2008 October 29—the suspended Game Five (caused torrential rain) is resumed and the Phillies defeat the Rays, 4–3, thus gaining their second World Series victory. A record crowd of 45,940 watches.
2009 October 21—by beating the Dodgers 10–4 to win the National League Championship, the Phillies advance to the World Series to defend their 2008 title. 46,214 watch.
2009 November 2—the Phillies win Game 5 of the World Series against the Yankees 8–6 but go on to lose the next game 7–3 and the series 4–2.

Philadelphia has had the best of ballparks, and the worst of ballparks. Now it has a relatively new one. Citizens Bank Park, opened in time for the 2004 season, is Philadelphia's edition of a throwback park, said to mimic stately Shibe Park, which was opened before World War I, and Baker Bowl, where the Phillies began playing baseball in the time of Mark Twain.

It is located across the street from Veterans Stadium, the run down cookie-cutter arena where the Phillies spent the last 30 years. The new park was tilted 45 degrees clockwise, in order to frame a panorama of downtown Philadelphia over its center-field wall. It has a natural grass infield and dirt basepaths, as compared to the artificial turf and small sliding pits in the Vet. It contains 20,000 fewer seats, and a concourse that allows fans to watch the action while they are walking around. The seats behind the plate are 10 feet closer than at the old stadium, and about half the seats are located below the concourse.

The outfield was loosely modeled after Shibe Park, which was best remembered for its enormous French Renaissance facade. Red steel, brick, and stone give the exterior a classic feel, and its main entrances are framed by light standards for a grand approach. Rising 50 feet above first, home, and third are glass towers which are illuminated at night. The field's distinctive shape, with a little lip in left field, is expected to create entertaining bounces. The architects conducted extensive wind studies, measuring ball trajectories and wind velocities which led them to conclude that Citizens Bank Park will be neither a hitter's nor a pitcher's park.

The center-field concession area is dedicated to Philly Hall of Famer and broadcaster Richie Ashburn. Greg "the Bull" Luzinski, who enjoyed many years of glory at the Vet, serves BBQ in Ashburn Alley, as Boog Powell does for Oriole fans at Baltimore's Camden Yards.

A statue of Connie Mack, the great Philadelphia A's player and manager has been brought over from the Vet. And inside the park, bronze statues honoring Phillies legends Mike Schmidt, Steve Carlton, Robin Roberts and Richie Ashburn celebrate past glories. A lot of emotional farewells were paid to the Vet in its final days, but the field at Citizens Bank Park was declared ready to go after the 2003 season amid high expectations—hopes that were justified within five years when the Phillies advanced to and won the 2008 World Series. The next year they reached the World Series again but failed narrowly to record back-to-back victories losing to the Yankees.

Considered one of the most hitter-friendly ballparks in MLB, in 2009 it saw 149 home runs, the most in the National League and second in the majors behind only the new Yankee Stadium that was going through an equally purple period. This certainly brought in the crowds—as did the Phillies excellent form—and that year the team set an all-time attendance record, attracting more than 3.5 million fans. However, poor recent form has seen a dropping off. In 2014 the Phillies finished in last place in the NLE and started 2015 with the worst record in baseball. The fans stayed away and at season's end only 1.8 million had passed through the turnstiles.

At the Phillies Star Walk the bricks were touched up for the 2017 season. Plus, the sign announcing "Ashburn's Alley" honoring Richie Ashburn at the entrances, was engraved onto the walkway.

Giveaways during the season included Jon Kruk jerseys, the ex-Phillie who once proclaimed, "I'm not an athlete, I'm a ballplayer." Also, a free cheese steak (the ultimate Philadelphia food) was scheduled to be given away to the first 500 fans one day.

In a move that some aficionados of both hobbies no doubt considered bizarre, but some no doubt embraced, the Phillies combined baseball cards and eating by selling a new 2017 set of trading cards featuring pictures of iconic ballpark foods. Meanwhile, in the actual eating world, the Phillies expanded the choice of items one might combine with a hot dog, the true ballpark staple food.

Right: Philadelphia Phillies pitcher Randy Wolf delivers the first pitch to Cincinatti Reds D'Angelo Jiminez in the new Citizens Bank Ballpark, April 12, 2004.
© Tim Shaffer/Reuters/Corbis

Left: Citizens Bank Park on April 3, 2014, five days before Opening Day. During the 2010–2011 off season $10 million was spent upgrading the video system around the facility: the old scoreboard was replaced with a massive HD scoreboard, 76ft high and 97ft wide, making it the largest in the National League. *Newyorkadam via WikiCommons*

Left: Veterans Stadium—the Phillies played baseball in "The Vet" for 32 years when it finally closed at the end of the 2003 season. Players and fans alike were ready to move on. The once-great stadium had seen its best days many years ago. The Vet's unique rounded rectangular shape has been the setting for two All-Star Games (1976, 1996) and three World Series (1980, 1983, and 1993).
National Baseball Hall of Fame

Left: Hall of Famers who wore a Phillies uniform and played at The Vet include Mike Schmidt, Joe Morgan, Tony Perez, and Steve Carlton.
National Baseball Hall of Fame

Right: Shibe Park in 1973 after abandonment; general view, looking NE.
Library of Congress, Prints & Photographs Division, PA-1738-1.

SHIBE PARK

SHIBE PARK (1909–70)

Home of the Philadelphia Athletics 1909–54
Home of the Philadelphia Phillies 1938–70

Just as Baltimore's Camden Yards would do eight decades later, Shibe Park touched off a baseball revolution. Steel-and-concrete, aesthetically pleasing, huge, and with attention to detail, the home of the Philadelphia Athletics and then the Phillies was widely imitated. Over the next five years, Ebbets Field, Forbes Field, Wrigley Field, Fenway Park, Braves Field, and Comiskey Park all opened, while still others were redone in concrete and steel. Beyond its distinctive field and enormous confines, Shibe was distinguished by its French Renaissance façade that belied the notion that it was a mere ballpark. Named in honor of the A's owner Ben Shibe, it was renamed Connie Mack Stadium in 1953. In 1971 the Phillies moved to Veterans Stadium, a park then hailed as modern, built in the mold of parks in St. Louis, Cincinnati and Pittsburgh. By the time of its last game in 2003, it was ridiculed as sterile and among baseball's worst parks.

WASHINGTON NATIONALS

NATIONALS PARK

Address:
1500 South Capitol Street, SE
Washington, D.C. 20003
Capacity: 41,313
Opening day: March 30, 2008—Atlanta Braves 2, Washington Nationals 3
Cost to construct: $611 million
Architect: Populous
Dimensions (ft):
Left Field—337
Left Center—377
Center Field—402
Right Center—370
Right Field—335
Defining feature: A grove of cherry blossoms located just beyond the left field bleachers.
All-Star Game: July 10, 2018 (projected)
Memorable moments:
2008 March 22—The George Washington University Colonials play the first game in Nationals Park defeating Saint Joseph's University 9–4.
2008 March 30—President George W. Bush threw the first pitch to Nationals' manager Manny Acta.
2009 July 27—Josh Willingham hits two grand slams in a game against the Milwukee Brewers, only the 13th player in MLB history to do this.
2009 October 4—victory in their final game gives the Nats the unusual honor of being the only team in MLB history to start a season with seven losses and end with seven wins.
2012 September 20—The Nats clinched their first playoff berth since moving to Washington, with a 4–1 win over the L.A. Dodgers. They then win the National League East but lose to the Cardinals in the playoffs,
2015, June 30—Right-hander Max Scherzer pitched a no-hitter to beat the Pittsburgh Pirates, 6-0. The only base runner was hit by a pitch in the ninth inning. Scherzer pitched a second no-hitter on October 3 that year, at New York's Citi Field.

When the American League transformed itself into a major league in 1901, the powers-that-be decided that the fledgling league needed a major presence on the East Coast, so in 1900 the Kansas City team moved to the capital and became the Washington Nationals or "Nats," more commonly known as the Senators.

Under the leadership of manager—and later owner—Clark Griffith, the Nats took the American League Championship in 1924 and 1925. One more title came in 1933, but over the next 26 years the Nats were destined to have just four more winning seasons. Griffith died in October 1955 and his son, Calvin, took over. He became convinced that a move was in the team's best interest, and after 1960 they moved to Minnesota and became the Twins.

The capital was not left without a major league baseball team because a new expansion Washington Senators debuted for the 1961 season. They, too, played at Griffith Stadium, but stayed for just one season, moving to the new D.C. Stadium, one of the first multipurpose "cookie cutter" stadiums, playing their first game there on April 9, 1962. In 1968 the facility was renamed RFK Stadium in honor of the assassinated Attorney General Robert F. Kennedy. The Senators shared the stadium, with the NFL's Washington Redskins, which used RFK until they moved into their own new FedEx Field in 1996.

The Senators were not a good baseball team. In their first four seasons they hit the century mark in losses and they used up five managers in just a decade. Financial problems and a dwindling fan base soon brought an end to the second Senators and 71 years of continuous major league baseball in the capital. They played their last game at RFK Stadium on September 30, 1971. The franchise moved to the Dallas-Fort Worth area and became the Texas Rangers.

It took more than three decades to bring baseball back to the nation's capital, but diehard fans were rewarded in 2005, when the former Montreal Expos made their home debut on April 15 as the reincarnated Washington Nationals. The Expos/Nationals had taken a bizarre route to the capital—including an aborted MLB plan to kill the franchise, and a stint playing part-time in Puerto Rico—but Washington fans enthusiastically welcomed the team.

The city invested more the $18.5 million upgrading RFK for baseball, and also agreed to build a new $535 million baseball-only stadium. After considerable political wrangling a site was selected at South Capitol and N streets SE, and the stadium—Nationals Park—opened for the 2008 season. The first sports facility in the U.S. to be Leadership in Energy and Environmental Design certified, it is a contemporary design with half of its seats on the lower deck nearer the action.

Marketing divisions seem to work overtime during the Major League off-season and the Nationals certainly fit that description. Maintaining allegiance to bobblehead collectors, Washington scheduled Daniel Murphy and Trea Turner bobblehead giveaway days for 2017. Also made available was a Magic 8-Ball, a promotional item no doubt fans lay awake dreaming of before Christmas.

Perhaps in a sneak preview of "luxury" boxes of the future, the team installed eight, cushiony, living-room-style black chairs in the stands that most definitely promise more comfort than the old days of hard, no-back bleacher seats.

In a new opportunity at the customization stand in the team store, fans purchasing new caps and even bringing in old ones, were able to choose their own favorite designs to be added.

Right: Nationals Park at twilight during their first home game in Washington, March 29, 2008. Four losing years followed and the initial enthusiasm for the ballpark waned. And then, miracle of miracles, under Davey Johnson things changed. In 2012 when they achieved the franchise's first postseason berth since 1981. A second followed under in 2014 under Matt Williams.
Jason Reed/Reuters/Corbis

Overleaf: Panorama of Nationals Stadium during the Nationals vs. Rangers game of June 22, 2008.
Brian Williams

Far Left: Griffith Stadium opened in 1911 and was home to the American League Senators through 1960, and to the expansion team Senators in 1961. It saw World Series games in 1924, 1925, and 1933, the Negro league Homestead Grays during the 1940s, and the NFL Washington Redskins of the National Football League (1937–1960).
National Baseball Hall of Fame

Left: A fisheye view of Washington Nationals game against the Cincinnati Reds on August 25, 2005, at RFK Stadium. The Reds defeated the Nationals 5–3.
MLB Photos via Getty Images

NATIONAL LEAGUE CENTRAL

The teams of the National League Central are among baseball's oldest. Baseball has been played in Chicago, Cincinnati, Pittsburgh, and St. Louis since the 19th century. However, the division's ballparks are also among the game's newest.

Chicago's Wrigley Field, opened in 1916, is the National League's oldest park, and in the eyes of many purists, baseball's best. The manual scoreboard, outfield wall ivy, and close confines have come to define the game. Seventy-five years after Wrigley was built, four National League Central division teams opened 21st century parks.

The Houston Astros replaced their fully enclosed Astrodome with a downtown, retractable-dome stadium in 2000. Pittsburgh moved into a new ball yard on the banks of the Allegheny River that some claim is every bit as pleasant as Wrigley. Milwaukee also opened a new park in 2001, replacing County Stadium, while Cincinnati moved from sterile Riverfront Stadium, later named Cinergy Field, to a new home in 2003. Not to be outdone, the St. Louis Cardinals built a new stadium (the third Busch Stadium) in time for the 2006 season, leaving Wrigley Field as the division's only 20th century park.

Right: View of the Great American Ball Park from home plate upper level during the game between the Cincinnati Reds and the Houston Astros.
Jerry Driendl/Getty Images

CHICAGO CUBS

WRIGLEY FIELD

Right: An undated photo showing Wrigley prior to the 1937 season when its signature bleachers were constructed. The alterations and enhancements made it one of the most pleasant places on earth to watch a ballgame.
National Baseball Hall of Fame

Aka: Weeghman Park (1914–15), Cubs Park(1916–26)
Address:
1060 West Addison
Chicago, IL 60613
Capacity: 41,268
Opening day: April 23, 1914—Chicago Federals 9, Kansas City Packers 1
Opening day: (Cubs) April 20, 1916—Chicago Cubs 7, Cincinnati Reds 6 (11 innings)
Cost to construct: $250,000
Architect: Zachary Taylor Davis
Dimensions (ft):
Left Field—355
Left Center—368
Center Field—400
Right Center—368
Right Field—353
Defining feature: Outfield ivy
Little-known ground rule: Baseball stuck in vines covering bleacher wall: Double
World Series: 1918, 1929, 1932, 1935, 1938, 1945, 2016
All-Star Game: 1947, 1962, 1990
Memorable moments:
1917 May 2—Chicago's Jim "Hippo" Vaughn and Cincinnati's Fred Toney both pitch 9 innings of no-hit ball, before Cincinnati's Jim Thorpe drives in the winning run in the 10th inning.
1932 October 1—Babe Ruth gestures toward the center field bleachers in the 5th inning of game three of World Series before hitting the ball there for his second home run of the game.
1945—The Cubs' last appearance in the World Series, the longest drought in the majors.
1988 August 8—The first night game at Wrigley Field.
2016, October 22—The Cubs clinched their first National League pennant by beating the Los Angeles Dodgers in the National League Championship Series.
2016, October 28—The first World Series game since 1945 was played at Wrigley as the Cubs took on the Cleveland Indians

Wrigley Field is what every baseball park wants to be. Simple, intimate, handsome, and distinct, cities and team owners around the country have spent hundreds of millions of dollars, hired architects, engineers, and historians, all hoping to recreate what has existed on Chicago's North side for a century.

Built on the grounds of a seminary in 1914, the park opened as Weeghman Park, home to the Chicago Federals (also known as the Whales) in the soon-to-be defunct Federal League. Two years later it was Cubs Park, when the National League team moved in, and then Wrigley Field when the chewing gum magnate took control of the team a decade later.

Change marked Wrigley's early years. A second deck was added in 1927. The signature bleachers and 27-foot high scoreboard were built in 1937. That same year, Bill Veeck planted hundreds of Boston Ivy plants along the outfield brick wall. A clock was added atop the scoreboard four years later. Since then, time has essentially stood still inside the "friendly confines" which Hack Wilson, Ernie Banks, Billy Williams, Fergie Jenkins, Ryne Sandberg, and Sammy Sosa have all called home.

Take a look at a picture of Wrigley in the early 1940s and another from today. The top hats and black jackets have been replaced by bright blue Cubbie caps and t-shirts and the high rises beyond center field have grown taller, but little else has changed. There were no billboards inside the park then, and there are none today.

The scoreboard is still hand-operated (and not large enough to accommodate every out-of-town game since the major leagues expanded.) After each Cub victory, a white flag with a blue W is raised high above the scoreboard, a white L on a blue flag indicates a loss, a system originally created to let Wrigley's neighbors keep track of their team long before the advent of sports tickers or ESPN.

Chicago baseball in the 21st century is much as it was prior to World War II, providing an incredible link to another era and one that ballparks from Baltimore to Seattle have tried to capture for themselves.

Wrigley Field, as the second oldest major-league park after Fenway, is the birthplace of many baseball traditions. It was the first place that allowed fans to keep balls hit into the stands. The first concession stands were built in the park's opening year, after patrons complained that roaming vendors were blocking their view. In 1941, the Cubs became the first team to play organ music in its ballpark. It is here that Harry Caray, leaning outside his broadcast booth with microphone in hand and beer poorly concealed behind the window, made famous the tradition of singing Take Me Out To The Ballgame during the seventh inning stretch which is now imitated wherever baseball is played.

Until 1988, Wrigley's most distinctive feature was its lack of lights. Team owners were ready to install them in time for the 1942 season when the U.S. was attacked at Pearl Harbor. The day after the attack, team owner P.K. Wrigley donated the equipment to the War Department. Lights were finally erected in 1988 after league officials threatened to hold Cubs postseason games at the home of the rival Cardinals in St. Louis. Wrigley's first night game, in what some saw as an omen, was suspended in the fourth inning after a torrential downpour. The first official game was played the following night when the Cubs beat the Mets 6 to 4.

After thousands of games, no baseball has yet hit the center-field scoreboard, though a towering home run hit onto Sheffield Avenue by Bill Nicholson in 1948, and another one hit onto Waveland Avenue in 1959 by Roberto Clemente, barely missed. Sam Snead reached the scoreboard with a golf ball, prior to a game in 1951.

Cub fans are familiar with many smaller changes over the years. Luxury boxes have been added to bring in revenue, and in 1970 a basket was installed along the bleachers to keep fans from interfering with balls. Seats have been erected on the rooftops along Waveland and Sheffield Avenues, where more casual viewing was once a tradition.

Yet Wrigley baseball looks much the same today as it did when Zip Zabel came in to pitch 18 innings in relief over Brooklyn in 1915, when Stan Musial collected his 3,000 hit, when

Ernie Banks hit his 512th and final home run, when Fergie Jenkins pitched his 3,000 strikeout, and when Pete Rose tied Ty Cobb with hit No. 4,191.

After winning their first World Series crown since 1908, the Chicago Cubs could probably do whatever they wanted with Wrigley Field and fans would keep the smiles on their faces. In one form or another Wrigley has been around since 1914, but before 2016 it had not hosted a World Series game since 1945.

Through constant expansion management has squeezed in a handful of seats anywhere it could, and its size is now more in line with the typical park. For years, when the Cubs were regularly finishing near the bottom of the National League standings, the ballpark itself was an attraction. In 2016, the No. 1 attraction was the successful team.

The World Series championship happened to come along when the Cubs were in the midst of a gradual series of park upgrades spread over several seasons. Even if a fan attended the last home game of 2016, he was greeted by something new in 2017, as if the euphoria of being the defending world champ wasn't enough, especially the hoisting of a World Series championship flag on opening day of 2017. Winning trumps all.

Also added was a new west side gate, a Starbucks, an eating and drinking stand-around plaza and bullpens moved out of view, replacing a century's worth of warming up on the sidelines. Under the bleachers went the relief core.

After catering to the most patient fans in the sports universe, Cubs management rewarded them in 2017. As part of the coolest giveaways in sports, the first 30,000 fans on April 12 were given replicas of the championship banner and on April 15 the first 10,000 fans were given replicas of the World Series trophy.

Left: Exterior view of Wrigley Field during the game between the Philadelphia Phillies and the Chicago Cubs on July 23, 2003.
Jerry Driendl/Getty Images

Above: Wrigley Field from a right field skybox across the street from the ballpark during the game between the Phillies and the Cubs on July 23, 2003. The large gate in right field is there specifically for the traveling circus that Wrigley used to regularly host, as an entrance for the elephants.
Jerry Driendl/Getty Images

Right: An aerial view of Wrigley Field. Easy to see why even the players refer to this classic park as the "Friendly Confines." By the time this photo was taken the bleachers and a second level of seats had been added to meet fan demand.
National Baseball Hall of Fame

Right: Wrigley Field's center-field scoreboard during the game between the Phillies and the Cubs on July 23, 2003.
Jerry Driendl/Getty Images

Inset: The ivy and scoreboard were introduced to Wrigley Field by Bill Veeck in 1937.
National Baseball Hall of Fame

Above: A view of Wrigley Field and the Wrigleyville neighborhood during batting practice before the Cubs–Angels game on June 18, 2010. Some of the houses in the area have rooftop bleachers—the so-called Wrigley Rooftops from which people can watch the games
Bspangenberg via WikiCommons (CC BY-SA 3.0)

Right: Chicago Cubs' fans watch a replay of Game 7 of the World Series on opening night, Monday, April 10, 2017. Played at Progressive Field on November 2, 2016, the last game of that World Series had everything: the Cubs' first postseason triumph for 108 years; a come-from-behind (Cleveland had led the series 3–1), extra-innings victory where either side could have won; and a seventeen-minute rain break after the ninth, with the game tied to heighten the tension.

"The Park at Wrigley" is the latest stage in the 1060 Project, which began in October 2014 and has seen major improvements to Wrigley Field—and will continue to develop the ballpark for the next three years. The Cubs want to open the plaza to all-comers on game days, something the city as yet won't allow.
Brian Cassella/Chicago Tribune/TNS via Getty Images

Left: Wrigley Field with Ron Santo No. 10 flags on the roof August 10, 2012, the day the statue of the Cubs' great was presented to the ballpark.
TonyTheTiger via WikiCommons (CC BY-SA 3.0)

CINCINNATI REDS

GREAT AMERICAN BALLPARK

Address:
100 Main Street
Cincinnati, Ohio 45202.
Capacity: 42,319
Opening day: March 31, 2003—Pittsburgh Pirates 10, Cincinnati Reds 1
Cost to construct: $290 million
Architect: HOK Sports
Dimensions (ft):
Left Field—328
Left Center—379
Center Field—404
Right Center—370
Right Field—325
Defining feature: "The Gap" in seats down the left field line
Most expensive seat: $225
Cheapest seat: $5
World Series: None
All-Star Game: 2015
Memorable moments:
2003 March 31—Former President George Bush, filling in for his son, President George W. Bush, throws out the ceremonial first pitch on the park's opening day.
2003 April 4—Sammy Sosa hits his 500th home run.
2003 July 21—Russell Branyan hits the stadium's first grand slam.
2004 September 25—Cincinnati Reds Hall of Fame opens next to Great American Ball Park.
2006 April 3—President George Bush becomes the first sitting president to throw out the first pitch at a Reds game.
2008 June 8—Ken Griffey, Jr. hits his 600th home run.
2010 October 10—First postseason game in the GABP sees the Phillies shutout the Reds 2–0.
2013 July 2—The first no-hitter at the GABP, by Reds' pitcher Homer Bailey.

Professional baseball began in Cincinnati. From the Union Cricket Club Grounds, where the Cincinnati Red Stockings first played in 1869, the Bank Street Grounds, where ladies had their own entrance, Crosley Field, where baseball had its first night game, to Riverfront Stadium where Hank Aaron tied Babe Ruth for the all-time home run record and Pete Rose passed Ty Cobb for baseball's all-time hit lead, the city on the banks of the Ohio River has always been a baseball town.

Cincinnati's latest park, opened in 2003, hopes to play off the tradition. The scoreboard clock is a replica of the one that once sat in Crosley Field. The main entry and even the seats were designed to resemble the old park. A rose garden is being grown outside the stadium itself, on the very spot where Pete Rose's record 4,192nd hit landed in old Riverfront Stadium.

At the same time, this is a thoroughly modern park, where season tickets to the cushioned seats just 50 feet from home plate ("closer to the batter than the pitcher," the team boasts) with special access to food and drink, sell for more than some players' annual salaries in baseball's not too distant past.

After sharing a home with the Bengals for 30 years at circular Riverfront Stadium, the Reds new home is built exclusively for baseball. It features an imposing, 68-foot high, 217-foot wide scoreboard, which is one of the major's largest.

The Great American Ballpark's signature feature is "The Gap" down the 3rd base line. The unique break in the seating makes for better angles and proximity to the field for seats down the line, opens up views of downtown for those inside the park, and lets passing pedestrians on the outside catch a glimpse of the field.

The exterior is brick with cast stone and painted steel, intended to reflect the architecture of Cincinnati and the nearby Roebling Suspension Bridge which crosses the Ohio River into Kentucky. Views of the river add to the park's character, but it would take a 580-foot shot to deposit a home run into the water. Among the park's other features is a statue of slugger Ted Kluzinski carry a bat on his shoulder like a lumberjack's ax, and a pair of smokestacks which shoot fireworks when a Reds player homers

The Great American Ballpark has fewer of the "retro" touches featured in new parks in Baltimore, Denver, San Francisco, or Pittsburgh. A panel of six architects shown the stadium by the Cincinnati Enquirer a week before it opened ripped the stadium as fragmented, erratic, and failing to provide either continuity or order.

The ballpark's name comes from the Great American Insurance company, which bought the naming rights for 30 years at a price of $75 million. Few changes were made to the Ball Park until 2009 when Daktronics replaced the scoreboards with new HD video displays. However for the 2015 MLB All-Star Game the Reds allocated $5 million for general improvements: these included two new bars and upgraded concession stands.

The Reds piled on the ballpark changes for 2017, although almost all were designed to appeal to fan eating or visual appetites as compared to configuration of the playing field. The JACK Casino Super Suite opened as the only field-level suite behind third base and is capable of holding as many as 40 people. The Scouts Club was renovated and saw a full-service bar installed—and private rest rooms.

A second All-You-Can-Eat stand was unveiled in right field. The Frontgate Outdoor Luxury Suite was expanded to hold groups of up to 48. A Frisch's Big Boy statue now stands in front of a third-base concessions stand, as opposed to a new statue of a Frank Robinson or another Reds Hall of Famer. Asian grilled sandwiches, Cheetos popcorn and Greater's Ice Cream joined the menu.

Above Right: The grandstand viewed from the outfield June 8, 2013. The 90–72 season ended with a wild card spot and a playoff loss to the Pirates.
Matthew Pintar

Right: The Cincinnati skyline at dusk during a game between the Astros and the Reds.
Jerry Driendl/Getty Images

Right: View from home plate upper level showing the great views of the Ohio and its paddleboats.
Jerry Driendl/Getty Images

Another night view. The suspension bridge is the Roebling Suspension Bridge, erected in 1866 as the Covington and Cincinnati Bridge and renamed after its designer John A. Roebling. *Jerry Driendl/Getty Images*

Above: Aerial view of the then Riverfront Stadium. It would be renamed Cinergy Field in 1996 after Cincinnati's electric company paid $6 million for the privilege.
National Baseball Hall of Fame

Left: Spectators aboard boats floating on the Ohio River watch as Cinergy Field is imploded on December 29, 2002, to make room for the nearby Great American Ballpark (on the right). More than 1,200lb of explosive material was used.
Mike Simons/Getty Images

MILWAUKEE BREWERS

MILLER PARK

Address:
One Brewers Way
Milwaukee, WI 53214
Capacity: 42,200
Opening Day: April 6, 2001—Milwaukee Brewers 5, Cincinnati Reds 4
Cost to construct: $400 million
Architect: HKS, Inc. (Dallas), NBBJ (L.A.), Eppstein Uhen Architects (Milwaukee)
Dimensions (ft):
Left Field—344
Left Center—371
Center Field—400
Right Center—374
Right Field—345
Defining feature: Bernie Brewer
World Series: None
All-Star Game: 2002
Memorable moments

2001 April 6—President Bush throws out the ceremonial first pitch, and the Brewers rally behind Richie Sexson's eighth-inning home run to beat the Cincinnati Reds in Miller Park's debut.

2002 July 10—The American and National leagues battle to a 7–7 All-Star game tie. Baseball Commissioner Bud Selig is booed for 30 minutes after announcing that the game would not continue because both teams had run out of pitchers.

2003 July 9—Pittsburgh outfielder Randall Simon is lead away in handcuffs after belting a costumed, 19-year-old woman participating in the sixth inning sausage race, with a baseball bat.

2006 July 29—The chorizo joins the bratwurst, the Italian, the Polish, and the hot dog in the sausage race. It will become a full-time member in 2007.

2008—The Brewers reached postseason play for the first time since losing the World Series in 1982.

2011 October 7—The Brewers beat the Diamondbacks 3–2 for their first playoff series win since 1982.

After playing for 30 years in County Stadium, a ballpark as plain as its name, the Brewers opened the new millennium in a park with all the latest bells and whistles.

Miller Park is the major leagues' latest retractable dome stadium, this one built in a unique fan shape, in which the 12,000-ton roof pivots around a point near home plate, covering more than 10 acres, and able to open and shut in just over 10 minutes.

The convertible structure not only means year-round climate control in a northern climate where April and September are pushing the baseball envelope, it also strikes wonder in the upper Midwest cheeseheads, who shattered attendance records in the park's first year. During the opening season, fans stuck around after the game on nice summer nights to watch the roof close to the symphonic sounds of Johann Strauss' "Blue Danube Waltz."

The stadium took almost five years to build, opening a year late after a tragic crane accident in 1999 killed three steel workers, and added $100 million to the project's cost.

The roof stands more than 30 stories high at its peak, adding an imposing new landmark to Milwaukee's modest skyline. The Brewers claim on their internet site, rather oddly, that the stadium weighs the equivalent of 62.5 million bowling balls, and that it would take 4.66 billion baseballs to fill it top to bottom.

Architects boast that the roof's steel mirrors the bridges over the Menomonee River, though the height of the walls and the omnipresence of the dome has led fans to complain that it feels like an indoor stadium even when the roof is open.

Patrons in County Stadium got to watch the project from their seats, as it was built just beyond centerfield in what was a parking lot. It includes a manual scoreboard and seats close to the field in the vain of other recent parks. Brewer Hall of Famer Robin Yount helped design the park's dimensions, which includes a quirky outfield with unique slants and angles.

Outside is a classic brick facade, with statues of Yount and Hank Aaron.

The Brewers transplanted some of their most distinctive traditions from County Stadium, including Bernie Brewer, who used to slide down an enormous, several-story high slide into a beer stein, and now does the same onto a platform in left field. Humans dressed in sausage costumes race around the bases in the middle of the sixth inning. And huge parking lots facilitate Wisconsin's obsession with tailgate parties.

Outside, eight names have been immortalized on a "Walk of Fame," that encircles the ballpark plaza, including Aaron, Yount, Rollie Fingers, Cecil Cooper, Paul Molitor, Allan H. (Bud) Selig, Harry Dalton and Bob Uecker.

The stadium offers $1 "Ueker seats," named after the well known Brewer's broadcaster, obstructed by roof pivots and located in the upper deck terrace, but still one of the best deals in baseball. A 2005 fan survey by *Sports Illustrated* rated Miller Park the best value ballpark based on dollar value.

During the off-season 2010–2011 the PA and sound system was upgraded and the centerfield scoreboard was replaced by a Daktronics 1080p HD display board.

The Brewers performed a complete overhaul of their concessions stands leading into the 2017 season. The contents were expanded with local foods and brands and a uniform design was implanted on the signage around Miller Park. Also introduced were 11 new concession stands on the first-base and third-base field level sides.

Right: A view of the entrance to Miller Park before the game between the Milwaukee Brewers and the Cincinnati Reds on May 17, 2003. The Brewers defeated the Reds 8–6.
Jonathan Daniel/Getty Images

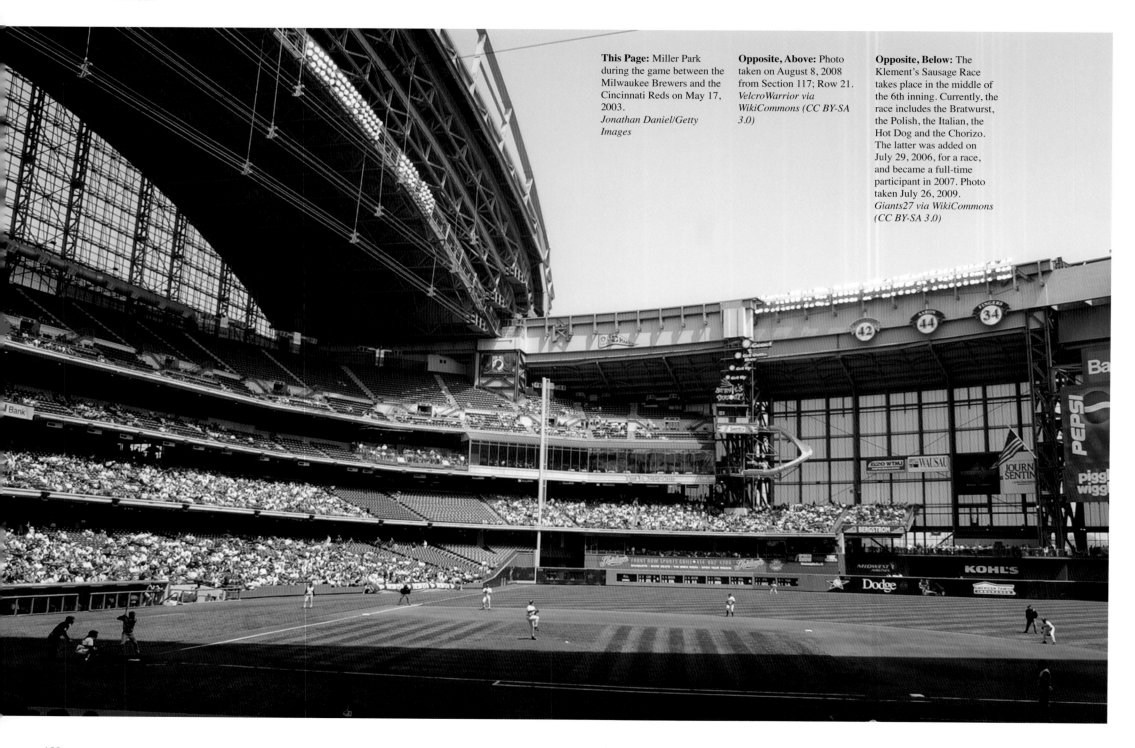

This Page: Miller Park during the game between the Milwaukee Brewers and the Cincinnati Reds on May 17, 2003.
Jonathan Daniel/Getty Images

Opposite, Above: Photo taken on August 8, 2008 from Section 117; Row 21.
VelcroWarrior via WikiCommons (CC BY-SA 3.0)

Opposite, Below: The Klement's Sausage Race takes place in the middle of the 6th inning. Currently, the race includes the Bratwurst, the Polish, the Italian, the Hot Dog and the Chorizo. The latter was added on July 29, 2006, for a race, and became a full-time participant in 2007. Photo taken July 26, 2009.
Giants27 via WikiCommons (CC BY-SA 3.0)

Satellite view of Miller Park on June 8, 2007. *USGS/NASA via WikiCommons*

MILWAUKEE COUNTY STADIUM (1953–2000)
Home of the Milwaukee Braves (1953–1965)
Home of the Milwaukee Brewers (1970–2000)

Unless you count the man who slid into a beer stein after each Brewer home run, there were few frills at Milwaukee County Stadium. The straight-forward ballpark was made exclusively for baseball, and the fans who sang "Beer Barrel Polka" during the seventh-inning stretch rarely complained. It is here that Hank Aaron started his remarkable career, and where Warren Spahn enjoyed nine, 20-win seasons. County Stadium was home to the Braves when they moved from Boston in 1953, and was a National League park for 13 seasons until their departure for Atlanta 13 years later. The American League Brewers moved in before the 1970 season (and 27 years before their return to the National League.)

Left: Milwaukee County Stadium in the 1950s. Milwaukee Journal/*National Baseball Hall of Fame*

Right: Milwaukee County Stadium from behind the right field foul post. Milwaukee Journal/*National Baseball Hall of Fame*

PITTSBURGH PIRATES

PNC PARK

Address:
115 Federal Street
Pittsburgh, PA 15212
Capacity: 38,602
Opening day: April 9, 2001—Cincinnati Reds 8, Pittsburgh Pirates 2
Cost to construct: $262 million
Architect: HOK Sports
Dimensions (ft):
Left Field—325
Left Center—383
Center Field—399
Right Center—375
Right Field—320
Defining feature: Roberto Clemente Bridge
World Series: None
All-Star Game: 2006
Memorable moments:

2001 June 27—Pirates Manager Lloyd McClendon steals first base, literally, after being ejected from the game for disputing a call at first base. Play is resumed after a replacement base is installed.

2001 July 28—Brian Giles hits a grand slam to cap a two-out, seven-run rally in the bottom of the ninth inning to beat the Astros 9–8.

2002 July 6—Houston's Daryle Ward becomes the first player to hit a home run into the Allegheny River over the park's right field wall, estimated at 479ft.

2010 April 27—Pirates break a 22-game losing streak at Miller Park when they beat the Brewers 7–3.

2013 October 1—in the National League Wild Card Game and in front of a record crowd of 40,629, the Pirates beat the Cincinnati Reds 6–2: their first post season victory since 1992.

2016, June 19—Former big-league pitcher-turned-broadcaster Bob Walk fell out of his seat testing the back of his chair while on air, his feet flying into the air and showing off dark socks on his shoeless feet.

2017, May 20. The Pirates gave fans a Bob Walk Announcer Chair-Tip Bobblechair, depicting him leaning back in the chair during the 2016 incident.

The nation's ultimate boutique park is located in its Iron City. At first glance, PNC Park looks like something out of a child's baseball fantasy. The outfield wall reveals sweeping views of the Allegheny River, the Depression-era Roberto Clemente bridge, riverboats, and downtown Pittsburgh. The stadium's simple two-deck construction and limited seating make it perhaps the most intimate park in the major leagues. Old-fashioned light standards add to the historic feel, while a huge scoreboard updates every game in baseball. Fans can arrive by riverboat, or by walking across the picturesque suspension bridge from downtown, which is closed to vehicles on game days.

If Camden Yards began the retro park revolution in 1992, Pittsburgh's PNC Park perfected it nine years later. Located on the north bank of the Allegheny River between the Roberto Clemente and the Fort Duquesne bridges, the park was built to show off Pittsburgh, where baseball has been played since the days when steel was produced for locomotives, not automobiles.

Located only blocks from where Three Rivers Stadium once stood, PNC Park is everything the old stadium wasn't—natural, intimate, and inviting. PNC is the first major-league park with just two decks to be built since Milwaukee County Stadium a half a century before it. As a result, it highest seat is just 88 feet from the field. Nearly three-quarters of the seats are on the field level. Fenway is the only major-league park with a smaller capacity.

Though many touches are borrowed from Forbes Field, where the Pirates played for 61 years, the view more resembles Exposition Park, which opened in 1882, and featured a view of barges floating down the Allegheny and Monongahela Rivers, not to mention smokestacks in the background.

The field dimensions are unique, with a nook in deep left that is 10 feet deeper than straight-away center. The outfield fences vary in height, ranging from just six feet in left field to 21 feet in right, honoring Clemente who wore No. 21.

The waters of the Allegheny are 443 feet, 4 inches from home plate, considerably further than McCovey Cove in San Francisco, but reachable on rare occasion by the game's most powerful left handed hitters. There is a walkway between the water and the park that gives fans views of the city and river, and a free look inside the park.

PNC Park relies on dark blue Pennsylvania steel, rather than the green more familiar in other new stadium. The distinctive light standards are modeled after those at Forbes Field. Outside, a statue of Honus Wagner, which first stood outside Forbes Field and later Three Rivers, is at the home plate entrance. The Roberto Clemente statue was moved to the foot of his bridge, and a new Willie Stargell statue greets visitors at the left field entrance. A statue for Bill Mazeroski was added at the right field entrance during the 2010 season—the 50th anniversary of the Pirates' 1960 World Series, which Mazeroski clinched with a Game 7 walk-off home run at Forbes Field.

Although PNC has the smallest capacity in the majors it wasn't very long ago that many seats were empty. The recent, few-year resurgence of the Pirates has ensured many sell-out days at the park. Some 240 seats were added between the end of the 2016 season and the start of the 2017 campaign. The extra seating appeared when the team removed several camera areas near home plate and on the third base-line. Also a new LED scoreboard was installed in right field and many luxury suites were renovated. A substantial number of cakes and desserts were introduced for those not satiated by giant hot dogs and burgers.

Right: A June 24, 2001, view of what is commonly regarded as one of the best ballparks in the world, with a wonderful view of the river and downtown Pittsburgh. Until 2013, the view was better than what was happening on field as the Pirates endured a dreary run of losing seasons in their new home. All that changed in 2013 and the Pirates have enjoyed the thrill of postseason baseball since then.
Rick Stewart/Allsport via Getty Images

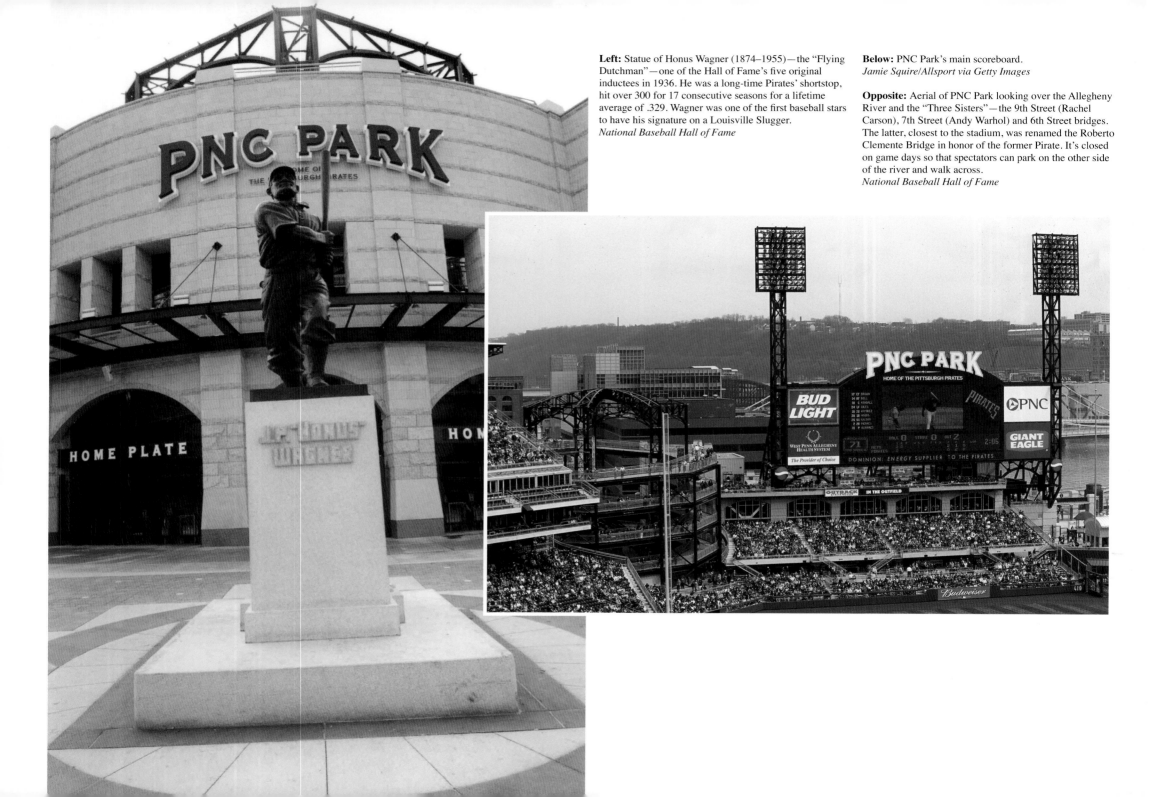

Left: Statue of Honus Wagner (1874–1955)—the "Flying Dutchman"—one of the Hall of Fame's five original inductees in 1936. He was a long-time Pirates' shortstop, hit over 300 for 17 consecutive seasons for a lifetime average of .329. Wagner was one of the first baseball stars to have his signature on a Louisville Slugger.
National Baseball Hall of Fame

Below: PNC Park's main scoreboard.
Jamie Squire/Allsport via Getty Images

Opposite: Aerial of PNC Park looking over the Allegheny River and the "Three Sisters"—the 9th Street (Rachel Carson), 7th Street (Andy Warhol) and 6th Street bridges. The latter, closest to the stadium, was renamed the Roberto Clemente Bridge in honor of the former Pirate. It's closed on game days so that spectators can park on the other side of the river and walk across.
National Baseball Hall of Fame

Left and Below: Three Rivers Stadium was imploded on February 11, 2001. Built where the Allegheny, Monongahela, and Ohio Rivers come together, a cookie-cutter stadium resembling those in Philadelphia, Cincinnati, and St. Louis, Three Rivers was home to the Pirates as well as the NFL Steelers.
Time Life Pictures/Getty Images

THREE RIVERS STADIUM (1970–2000)
Home of the Pittsburgh Pirates

Ground breaking started in 1968 for the replacement to Forbes Field, at the meeting point of the Allegheny and Monongahela rivers where they form the Ohio. As with Forbes, their new home saw immediate success for the Pirates: they were World Series champions in 1971 and again in 1979. Once the euphoria died down, however, the Pirates were left with a cookie-cutter stadium that could seat 58,729 from 1990, but rarely did. Discussions about a replacement started in the early 1990s and PNC Park was approved in 2008. The last MLB game at Three Rivers took place on October 1, 2000, and the stadium was imploded the next year.

Left: On May 25, 1935, at Forbes Field Babe Ruth hit the last home run of his major-league career. The blast cleared the right-field wall, then cleared the screen and finally cleared the double-deck grandstands. The historic shot (a first of that distance in Forbes Field) was approximately 86 feet high and at least 300 feet away from home plate. *National Baseball Hall of Fame*

FORBES FIELD (1909–71)
Home of the Pittsburgh
Pirates

Opened in Oakland on June
30, 1909, with a capacity
of 25,000, Forbes Field
was constructed of concrete
and steel with a three-tier
grandstand and roof box-
es—and ivy-covered walls.
The Pirates won their first
World Series there in 1909
and would win two more, in
1925 and 1960. The seating
was expanded to 35,000 in
1925, and it was considered
the best ballpark in league
in its early years. By the
time it was demolished,
however, it was long in the
tooth and although the 1960
season would see 1.7 million
visitors, plans were drawn
up to build a more modern
stadium in an area with more
parking. The last MLB game
at the ballpark was on June
28, 1971. Demolished in
1972, today, it lies under the
campus of the University of
Pittsburgh.

Left: Forbes Field was
remarkably well-laid out,
with landscaped gardens and
statues.
*National Baseball Hall of
Fame*

ST. LOUIS CARDINALS

BUSCH STADIUM

Address:
700 Clark Street
St. Louis, MO 63102
Capacity: 46,861
Opening day: April 10, 2006—St. Louis Cardinals 6, Milwaukee Brewers 4
Cost to construct: $400 million
Architect: HOK Sport (now Populous)
Dimensions (ft):
Left Field—336
Left Center—375
Center Field—400
Right Center—375
Right Field—335
Defining feature: Signature green fencing and red seats kept; statues from old stadium re-erected.
World Series: 2006, 2011
All-Star Game: 2009
Memorable moments:

2006 October 14—The Cardinals win the first of the NLCS games beating the Mets 5–0. They take the series 4–3.

2006 October 24, 26, and 27—Three World Series home games see three victories for the Cardinals over the Tigers and a 4–1 series triumph.

2011 October 27—With the Rangers leading the series 3–2, one of the greatest games ever sees the Cardinals become the first team to come back from deficits in both the 9th and 10th innings, They win the game 10–9 and go on to win the World Series.

2013 October 26—The Cardinals beat the Red Sox to take a 2–1 lead in the World Series. It's the high point of their campaign. They lose the next three games and the series.

2015, August 10—Infielder Matt Carpenter was on such a hot streak at the plate pitcher Carmelo Martinez splashed water on him as a joke.

2017, April 29—The Reds gave away a bobblehead of Carmelo Martinez splashing Matt Carpenter in the face with water.

When baseball elitists talk about a "cookie-cutter" stadium, they were talking about the old Busch Stadium built in 1966, opening just six months after the city's Gateway Arch on the banks of the Mississippi several blocks away. The Cardinals played their last game there on October 19, 2005, and moved into a new $400 million stadium—of course named Busch Stadium—for 2006.

HOK Sport designed a retro-looking arena in brick and steel but were equally interested in paying tribute to the previous Busch Stadium. Statues from the latter were re-erected at various points around the new stadium— that of Cardinals' legend Stan Musial can be found outside the third base entrance, for example. The old stadium's scoreboard can be seen on the main concourse and the traditional green fencing and red seats have been maintained. Embedded in the exterior sidewalk are fan-purchased inscribed bricks that surround marble plaques celebrating 100 great moments in the Cardinals' history.

The Cardinals became one of baseball's glory teams between the mid-1920s and mid-1940s when they captured nine NL pennants—1926, 1928, 1930, 1931, 1934, 1942, 1943, 1944, and 1946—and six World Series titles. During the 1960s, they had three World Series teams—1964, 1967, and 1968—and they returned to the World Series three times in the 1980s. They advanced to the playoffs only once in the 1990s, losing the championship series to the Braves in 1996, but things improved with the new millennium with five postseason appearances 2000–2005 including a World Series in 2004, where they were swept by the Red Sox.

Imagine the joy, therefore, when the first season in the new Busch Stadium saw a home World Series victory—the first time this had happened since 1923.

With such a long and successful history, it is hardly surprising that many Cardinals have made it to the Hall of Fame—nineteen in total. Perhaps the franchise's greatest player of all time (or at least the one most connected with the team) was Stan "The Man" Musial, a Cardinal from 1941 to 1963. He won the Most Valuable Player award in 1943, 1946, and 1949, led the league in hitting seven times, and played in 21 All-Star games. So popular and influential a figure was Musial that a statue in his honor was unveiled outside the Busch Stadium in 1968; in 1969 he entered the Hall of Fame, in his first year of eligibility.

With dramatic views of the Gateway Arch and the downtown St. Louis skyline, a red brick exterior, expanded bleacher sections, a state-of-the art video board, and knowledgeable fans, the new Busch Stadium is a great place to watch ball—and recent seasons have seen some great games: the 2009 All-Star Game; the 2011 World Series victory, including what some have called the greatest game in baseball history; 2012 postseason games against the Nationals and the Giants; and nine more in 2013. Spectator levels have been consistently high, topping three million, with the 2013 average of 41,602 the second best in the league.

To increase the size of the "Cardinal Nation," completed in time for Opening Day 2014 was Phase One of the St Louis Ballpark Village. This ambitious $650 million development occupies the site of the old Busch Stadium. Including the Cardinals Hall of Fame and Museum and the Busch 2 Infield, it is a Cardinals' themed retail, residential, office, and entertainments area designed to attract fans year round.

The Cardinals were thinking safety in the off-season between the end of the 2016 season and the start of the 2017 season. In 2017, fans were banned from carrying backpacks into Busch Stadium because it was taking security too long to search them and was delaying foot traffic. All open containers were also banned. Sealed water bottles were still OK. In another safety move, the netting behind home plate to the dugouts was extended to protect against foul balls.

Right: The interior of Busch Stadium during the third game at the ballpark, between the Brewers and the Cardinals, on April 13, 2006. The Brewers won 4–3 in the 11th in front of 40,222. Note the Gateway Arch in the distance—designed by Eero Saarinen it opened in 1967.
Elsa/Getty Images

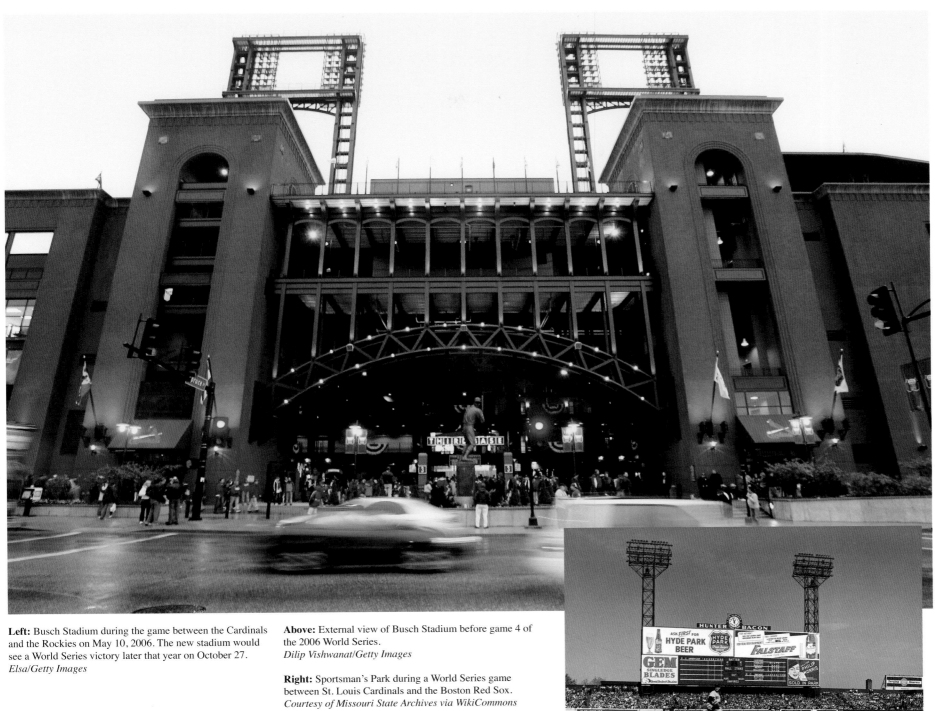

SPORTSMAN'S PARK
(1902–66)
Home of the St. Louis
Browns (AL) 1902-1953
Home of the St. Louis
Cardinals (NL) 1920-1966

Baseball has been played
on the corner of Grand and
Dodier since 1871. It was
in 1902 that Sportsman's
Park was built, which boasts
more major-league games
than any park in history. For
a remarkable 34 years, the
stadium was home to both
the Browns of the American
League and the Cardinals of
the National League. The two
teams met in the 1944 World
Series, with the Cardinals,
the more dominant team
during most of their joint
history, coming out on top.
This is the park where
Rogers Hornsby and Stan
Musial played, where a
goat in the 1940s helped
the grounds crew keep the
grass trim; where a midget
was sent up by team owner
Bill Veeck to draw a walk. It
was also the last park in the
majors to exclude African
Americans from its general
admission, providing them
seats in the 1940s in a right
field pavilion, which was
screened so no home run
balls could enter.
The Browns left for
Baltimore in 1953, and the
Cardinals moved into Busch
Stadium after the 1966
season. The grandstands are
gone, but baseball is still
played on the field where
Sportsman's once stood.

Left: Busch Stadium during the game between the Cardinals
and the Rockies on May 10, 2006. The new stadium would
see a World Series victory later that year on October 27.
Elsa/Getty Images

Above: External view of Busch Stadium before game 4 of
the 2006 World Series.
Dilip Vishwanat/Getty Images

Right: Sportsman's Park during a World Series game
between St. Louis Cardinals and the Boston Red Sox.
Courtesy of Missouri State Archives via WikiCommons

Main photo: Busch Stadium August 24, 2013, the year the Cardinals lost the World Series to the Red Sox.
Matthew Pinter

Inset: Busch Stadium as seen from the top of the Gateway Arch in May 2013.
ebgundy via WikiCommons (CC BY-SA 3.0)

Right: A panoramic view of the old Busch Stadium and nearby skyscrapers. This ballpark was demolished in 2005 to make way for the third stadium to bear the Busch name.
Joseph Sohm; ChromoSohm Inc./Corbis

NATIONAL LEAGUE WEST

The National League West includes two of baseball's most storied franchises, the Giants (1880s) and the Dodgers (1890s), who, like so many Americans, left their New York homes in the late 1950s for California. Unsurprisingly, both top the leaderboard of titles won (Dodgers 14, Giants 8); almost as many as the rest combined, including the three that left in 1993—the Reds, the Braves, and the Astros. The remaining three teams are relative babes— the Padres born in the 1960s, the Rockies in the 1980s, and the Diamondbacks in the 1990s.

The ballparks of the National League West have distinction. In AT&T Park, sluggers hit the ball into the San Francisco Bay. In Phoenix's Chase Field, they can hit the ball into a right-field swimming pool. In San Diego's Petco Park, batters smash balls off a left-field warehouse, while in Denver's Coors Field, they take advantage of the thin, mile-high air.

Los Angeles' Dodger Stadium, opened in 1962, is the division's only park built before 1995, and is still regarded as one of the best places in the division to watch a baseball game. The National League West is the only division in baseball where there is no talk of any team building a new park for many years to come.

Left: A general view of
Coors Field prior to the National League game between
the Arizona Diamondbacks
and the Colorado Rockies on
June 30, 2003.
Brian Bahr/Getty Images

ARIZONA DIAMONDBACKS

CHASE FIELD

Aka: Bank One Ballpark
Address:
401 E. Jefferson Street
Phoenix, AZ 85004
Capacity: 48,519
Opening day: March 31, 1998—Colorado Rockies 9, Arizona Diamondbacks 2
Cost to construct: $354 million
Architect: Ellerbe Becket
Dimensions (ft):
Left Field—330
Left Center—374
Center Field—407
Right Center—374
Right Field—334
Defining feature: Right field swimming pool
World Series: 2001
All-Star Game: 2011
Memorable moments:
1999 July 11—Jay Bell hits a grand slam in the sixth inning, winning $1 million for fan Gylene Hoyle, who had predicted the player and the inning in a pre-game contest.
2001 May 8—Randy Johnson strikes out 20 Reds to tie a major-league record, yet does not record a win. The Diamondbacks ultimately triumph 4–3 in 11 innings.
2001 October 28—The Diamondbacks beat the Yankees 4–0 to take a two games to none lead in the World Series as Randy Johnson throws a three-hit, complete game shutout.
2001 November 4—Luis Gonzalez hits a bases-loaded single to score Jay Bell, capping a two-run, ninth-inning comeback to beat the Yankees 3–2 in the seventh game of the World Series.
2006 March—Chase Field hosts three first-round games of the World Baseball Classic.

Chase Field is a monument to the power of air conditioning. The very qualities that make the Phoenix area such a popular destination for Cactus League games in the spring make it downright unbearable for baseball in the summer, when the average high temperature tops 100 degrees for three consecutive months.

Chase Field cools things down with 8,000 tons of air conditioning equipment, capable of creating enough cold air to chill 2,500 homes, and bring temperatures down by 30 degrees in three hours.

The unique retractable roof allows sunlight to shine on the natural turf, while keeping the oppressive desert heat from baking the grandstands. Nine million pounds of structural steel, using the same technology as a drawbridge, can open and close in less than five minutes, and can move into a variety of partially open positions.

More than 80 percent of the seats are located between the foul poles, and there is no upper deck in the outfield. Natural turf and an old-fashioned dirt path connecting the pitchers mound to home plate, give the park more of a classic feel than might be expected under a dome. Its most unique feature is the swimming pool and hot tub located just beyond the right field fence about 415 feet from home plate, where bathing suit clad patrons where bathing suit clad patrons can buy tickets for a swim and a unique outfield view. Chicago's Mark Grace was the first to plunk a ball into the pool in May of 1998, a feat that has since been achieved many times. Outside, Chase Field more resembles an airplane hanger than a baseball stadium. The red brick and green structural steel are said by the architects to blend into Phoenix's surrounding warehouse district, but the huge baseball murals on the side give it the look of a basketball or hockey arena.

Originally named Bank One Ballpark, or the "BOB," after Bank One merged with J.P. Morgan Chase & Co., the name change was announced on September 23, 2005.

Chase Field was still home when the 2017 baseball season began, but if the team has its way that relationship will end as soon as possible. The club wants a new ballpark. The Diamondbacks began demanding upgrades to the stadium or they'll leave Phoenix. Landlord Maricopa County has expressed a cooperative attitude to a point, indicating it is willing to sell the land where the ballpark resides to a developer if agreement can be reached on an alternative ballpark location. After a lot of legal threats backward and forward it turns out the groups had a mutual agreement that neither could sue the other, so the debate over the maintenance matter was sent to an arbitration mediator to solve. Still, it remains apparent the Diamondbacks are mostly interested in a long-term future in Arizona, but in a new park.

Above: Note the Ramtrucks.tv Pool in right field. Chase Field boasts a 385 square-foot warm water pool and an 85 square-foot hot tub.
User: (WT-shared) Jtesla16 at wts wikivoyage (detail)

Right: 2011 view of Chase Field from the corner of E Jefferson and South 4th Street. There's no sign of the roof, so it must be closed!
Cygnusloop99 via WikiCommons (CC BY-SA 3.0)

Left: The fantastic view from seats in Section 324 at Chase Field during a game between the D-backs and the Cardinals April 3, 2013. Daytime temperatures in Phoenix are usually in the 80s and 90s—so the roof is open.
Cygnusloop99 via WikiCommons (CC BY-SA 3.0)

Overleaf:
Left: General Manager Jerry Colangelo of the D-backs throws the ceremonial first pitch before his team plays the San Diego Padres during Opening Day at Bank One Ballpark April 1, 2002.
Donald Miralle/Getty Images

Right: Batting practice under the closed roof.
Digitalballparks.com

COLORADO ROCKIES

COORS FIELD

Address:
2001 Blake Street
Denver, CO 80205
Capacity: 50,398
Opening day: April 26, 1995—Colorado Rockies 11, New York Mets 9 (14 innings)
Cost to construct: $215 million
Architect: HOK Sports
Dimensions (ft):
Left Field—347
Left Center—390
Center Field—415
Right Center—375
Right Field—350
Defining feature: Row of purple, mile-high seats
World Series: 2007
All-Star Game: 1998
Memorable moments:
1995 October 1—The Rockies beat the Giants 10–9 and reach the NL playoffs in just their third season.
1996 September 12—Ellis Burks steals his 30th base of the season, a month after hitting his 30th home run, to join baseball's elite 30–30 club. Teammate Dante Bichette joins him by hitting his 30th home run the following night.
2003 April 10—First baseman Todd Helton snags a line drive off the bat of Cardinal Orlando Palmeiro, setting in motion the Rockies first triple play.
2007 October 6—Rockies win 2–1 to sweep the Phillies and win the NLDS 3–0...
2007 October 15—then win 6–4 to sweep Arizona and win the NLCS 4–0...
2007 October 28—but the Red Sox win the fourth game 4–3 and take the World Series.
2015—Nolan Arenado wins his third consecutive NL Golden Glove, the first third baseman to do so, after hitting 42 homers.
2016, April—Rookie shortstop Trevor Story tied the Major League record for most homers (10) by a rookie in April.

The purple seats on the 20th row of Coors Field's upper deck tell the story of this ballpark. It is there that the elevation reaches 5,280 feet, exactly one mile above sea level. At that altitude balls fly further. Curve balls break less sharply. And that, more than any other feature, has defined the Rockies' home.

Coors Field, the first park in the National League to be constructed exclusively for baseball since Dodger Stadium 33 years earlier, is by no means a small park. Its center field fence is a deep 415 feet, and left center juts out nine feet deeper. Yet the dimensions are deceptive. According to a team estimate, a ball hit 400 feet at sea-level Yankee Stadium would travel 440 feet in mile high Coors Field. The thin air contributed to a record-setting 1999 season, when teams combined for an average of 15 runs and four home runs each game.

The incredible offense, the classic charm of the old-fashioned park, and the views of the Rocky Mountains in the distance, have made Coors Field among the best attended parks in baseball history.

The deep red brick and Colorado sandstone exterior makes Coors Field look like it has always been located in Denver's lower downtown, on a spot where a train depot once stood. The classic architecture and old-fashioned corner front clock are reminiscent of Ebbets Field, and anchor a newly bustling downtown neighborhood.

Inside, the triple deck structure features small foul areas, an asymmetric field, and seats with sight lines geared toward the infield. A heating system under the field melts snow quickly, and its drainage system can clear away five inches or rain in a matter of hours.

The absence of an upper deck in left field provides fans along the first base and right field side a spectacular view of the Rocky Mountains. The stadium's designers passed up the chance to offer a panoramic view of downtown Denver so the sun would not be in batters' eyes, though the skyline is still visible from the top of the Rockpile, a 2,300-seat center field bleacher section where many tickets are held until game day, and kids and seniors can get in for just $1.

The park was originally designed to be even more intimate, seating just 43,000. But the huge popularity of baseball in nearby Mile High Stadium, where the Rockies played their first two years, persuaded the owners to add another 6,000 seats.

After the close of the 2013 season, the right field upper deck, converted into an outdoor party area for 2014. The Rooftop now features two decks with phenomenal views over the Rockies, bars, and rentable party spaces.

On March 29, 2017, just before the beginning of the new baseball season, the Colorado Rockies and the state's Metropolitan Baseball Stadium District agreed on a 30-year extension of the team's lease at Coors Field. After four years of negotiations, the Rockies agreed to pay $200 million as part of the long-term commitment to remain in Denver at Coors Field. As part of the arrangement, the Rockies gained the rights to develop land south of the ballpark for 99 years, paying $125 million for that privilege. The land was a parking lot at the time of the deal.

This agreement came just days before the team's 22-year lease at the Park was set to expire. There was a five-year rollover clause, but the Rockies wanted a more permanent solution.

Like many other ballparks, Coors seems to be in competition to offer the most outrageous food items at the concession stands, many of which will never be found at restaurants outside ballpark walls. New for 2017 were such foodstuffs as apple pie nachos, which actually began as a joke suggestion, candied bacon cream puffs, and Rock Pile Ale, brewed on-site.

Right: The Rockies play the Reds on July 25, 2015. A sad day for most fans, this was shortstop Tulo's (Troy Tulowitzki) final home game before he moved to the Blue Jays. A five-time MLB All-Star, he twice won the Gold Glove Award, three times the Fielding Bible, and twice the Silver Slugger.
Thelastcanadian via WikiCommons(CC BY-SA 4.0)

Left: July 1998 photo of the Rockies playing the Pirates. 3,792,683 people visited Coors Field in that year (the best ever was 1996 with 3,891,014) but recently the lack of a successful team has seen the annual average of over three million visitors dwindle to 2.5 million in 2015.
Joseph Sohm; ChromoSohm Inc./Corbis

Left: A view looking back over the diamond and downtown Denver taken during a game between the Braves and Rockies on June 18, 1995. A row of purple seats in the upper deck marks the elevation at exactly one mile above sea level.
Nathan Bilow/Allsport via Getty Images

Right: A view from right field over the diamond toward the Rocky Mountains: Coors Field has wonderful views from its substantial stands. The Rockies have only had seven winning seasons since formation in 1993: at least despairing fans have been able to enjoy the scenery.
Jonathan Daniel/Allsport via Getty Images

LOS ANGELES DODGERS

DODGER STADIUM

Address:
1000 Elysian Park Avenue
Los Angeles, CA 90012
Capacity: 56,000
Opening Day: April 10, 1962—Cincinnati Reds 6, Los Angeles Dodgers 3
Cost to construct: $23 million
Architect: Emil Praeger
Dimensions:
Left Field—330
Left Center—385
Center Field—395
Right Center—385
Right Field—330
Defining feature: Wavy roof over bleachers
Little-known ground rule: In its first year, the foul poles were mistakenly placed entirely in foul territory, and required special league dispensation to recognize balls that hit them as fair. Home plate was moved the following year to bring the poles into fair territory.
World Series: 1963, 1965, 1966, 1974, 1977, 1978, 1981, 1988
All-Star Game: 1980
Memorable moments:
1963 October 6—The Dodgers sweep the Yankees in the World Series.
1969 August 5—Pirate Willie Stargell hits a home run completely out of Dodger Stadium, a feat he would accomplish twice in his career.
1988 October 15—Hobbling pinch hitter Kirk Gibson hits a two-strike, two-out, two-run homer off Oakland's Dennis Eckersley to win game 1 of the World Series 5 to 4.
1995 August 10—The Dodgers forfeit a game against the Cardinals on "ball day" after a ninth-inning fracas which began with Raul Mondesi and manager Tommy Lasorda ejected for arguing with the home plate umpire, and ends when hundreds of souvenir balls bombard the umpires and Cardinal players.

Dodger Stadium isn't a "retro" park, nor does it pretend to be.

Five-tiered, perfectly symmetrical, and without a single deep red brick, Dodger Stadium sits atop Chavez Ravine as a testament to West Coast fans' affection for baseball.

At a time when old-fashioned, or neoclassical parks are the rage, Dodger Stadium stands out as the exception that proves there is more than one way to build a great baseball park.

For decades, what distinguished Dodger Stadium was its simplicity, its cleanliness, and its single-minded devotion to the game. Between the opening of Chicago's Wrigley Field in 1914 and Denver's Coors Field in 1995, Dodger Stadium was the only National League park built exclusively for baseball.

Dodger owner Walter O'Malley, who broke Brooklyn's heart by moving the Dodgers west, was given the site by the city of Los Angeles, who had evicted Mexican American residents from the hilltop for proposed public housing, creating Latino animosity toward the Dodgers that persisted for decades.

The wayward Angels also played at Dodger Stadium until their park in Anaheim was opened in 1966, preferring to call it Chavez Ravine so as not to advertise their crosstown rivals.

Deep power alleys have made this a pitchers' park, and Sandy Koufax, Don Drysdale, Fernando Valenzuala, and Orel Hershiser all thrived here. The grounds keeping is meticulous. More than 3,000 trees cover the 300-acre site, including several dozen trademark palm trees down the right and left field foul lines, which along with the Elysian Hills and the distant San Gabriel Mountains, give the park a distinctive Southern California look. The computer-controlled, Bermuda grass field, with state-of-the art vacuum chambers to assist draining, was rated No. 1 by baseball players in a Sports Illustrated survey in 2003.

The sight lines are on the mark, with no obstructed views. Each deck is freshly painted each season with its own color. Spectacular sunsets and the distinctive wavy roof over the bleachers give an instantly recognizable look to the stadium which was originally designed with the ability to expand to 85,000 seats, but has remained far smaller.

Dodger Stadium has hosted many events. Pope John Paul II celebrated mass there in 1987. The Beatles, the Rolling Stones, and the Three Tenors are among the long list of performers who have played on the field which also hosted Olympic baseball competition, the Harlem Globetrotters, boxing matches, and even a ski-jumping exhibition.

Over the past four decades the ballpark has been carefully improved. A video screen capable of showing instant replays, that debuted during the 1980 All-Star game, was baseball's first. Since 2000, the Dodgers have added new field level seats, and club suits, and a new state-of-the-art video screen. After the 2005 season all of the old seats were removed and replaced by new ones in yellow, light orange, turquoise, and sky blue. Ambitious plans to build a new Field Level concourse, with more concessions and restrooms, were completed in 2008.

In March 2012 Frank McCourt, owner since 2004, had to sell up to Guggenheim Baseball Management for $2.15 billion thanks to a much publicized divorce. There was talk of moving the franchise but the new management put its money down not only to improve the team but also for major improvements to the planned under the direction of stadium specialist Janet Marie Smith.

The effect on the team was immediate: the Dodgers won the Western Division title in 2013. The stadium also improved: for 2013 there were new HD hexagonal video boards, a new sound system, wider concourses, and more standing room viewing areas. For 2014, the investment of $150 million saw expansion of the entries at the field level, two new 25,000-square-foot plazas in right and left field; viewing areas overlooking the bullpens; a new walkway allowing fans on field level to do a 360-degree interior walk; a new state of the art wireless system throughout; enhancement of the ballpark's landscaping—the Three Sisters are back beyond the bullpen and more than 90 new trees are part of the new plaza area—and improved vehicular and pedestrian access.

Right: Dodger Stadium looks today much as it did when it opened in 1962. Dodgers fans enjoyed a rollercoaster for the first 26 years with eight appearances in the World Series, winning in 1963, 1965, 1981, and 1988 and losing in 1966, 1974, 1977, and 1978. Since then, there have been seven NL West Division titles, and eight post seasons but no World Series.
National Baseball Hall of Fame

On April 15, 2017, marking the 70th anniversary of Jackie Robinson's Major League debut, the Dodgers conducted a special ceremony outside the ballpark, unveiling a statue commemorating his achievements. Located outside of left field on a plaza, it is the first statue at Dodger Stadium. It portrays Robinson, the man who broke baseball's color barrier in the 20th century with a bold 1947 season, in mid-slide. One of the future Hall of Famer's most notable on-field traits was his daring on the base-paths. Robinson's name and his No. 42 were also engraved on the statue's base.

Every April 15, all players in the majors wear No. 42 for their games. Major League Baseball retired the No. 42 across the board for all teams with the exception of this day.

Those in attendance for the special occasion at Dodger Stadium were such team greats as Sandy Koufax, Don Newcombe (a Robinson teammate), Hall of Fame manager Tom Lasorda, Frank Robinson (baseball's first African-American manger) and Robinson's widow, Rachel Robinson, 94, and two living children.

Also for 2017, some new premium seating was installed, and the Dodgers put in place display cases of memorabilia highlighted by Vince Scully items in his first season in retirement, and venerable game-worn jerseys belonging to Jackie Robinson and Koufax.

Right: Another sellout crowd enjoys a game at Dodger Stadium. Three West Division titles under Don Mattingly in 2013–2015 boosted attendances to over 3.7 million
Robert Landau/Corbis

Left and Below: Dodger Stadium in 2012. Mattingly's second season saw the team 86–76 and second in the division in the ballpark's Golden Anniversary year. In contention for the playoffs until the last few games of the season, they beat the Giants who would go on to take the World Series 5–1 in their final game.
The Jon B. Lovelace Collection of California Photographs in Carol M. Highsmith's America Project, Library of Congress, Prints and Photographs Division

Below: The latest addition to Dodger Stadium is this bronze of Jackie Robinson, who grew up in Pasadena and met his wife at UCLA in 1941. He famously broke the color bar on April 15, 1947, when he started at first base for the then Brooklyn Dodgers. Robinson played for the Dodgers until he retired on October 10, 1956, the year before the team moved to Los Angeles. Sculpted by Oakland-based artist Branly Cadet, unveiled on Jackie Robinson Day, the bronze is the first of a planned series of sculptures honoring Dodgers' greats.
Victor Decolongon/Getty Images

EBBETS FIELD
(1913–57)
Home of the Brooklyn Dodgers

Ebbets Field is arguably where
baseball became the national
pastime. For 45 years, the
stadium between Brooklyn's
Bedford and Flatbush
neighborhoods defined what
it meant to go to the ballpark.
From its brick arched exterior
to its ornate domed rotunda,
many of today's stadiums reflect
its memory. Seats were close
to the field. The outfield wall
framed a uniquely shaped field.
Its trademark Shaefer Beer
billboard flashed an "H" for hits
and an "E" for errors. Clothier
Abe Stark invited players to hit
his advertisement on the outfield
fence for a free suit, something
he never needed to pay up.

It was here that Jackie
Robinson broke the color
barrier in 1947, where television
broadcast its first game, where
the Dodgers won nine pennants,
and where owner Walter
O'Malley broke Brooklyn's
heart by taking his team to Los
Angeles.

In its final years, O'Malley
complained that the stadium was
falling apart, and he searched
for a new home. He was not
satisfied with the plot of land
offered to him in Queens where
the Mets would end up several
years later. He left Brooklyn
for the west after the 1957
season. The wrecking balls
began demolishing the park in
1960. Today, the site is home to
a low-income housing project,
aptly named the Jackie Robinson
apartments.

Left: The classic lines of Ebbets Field seen during the 1956 World Series. On August 26, 1939, the first ever televised baseball game came from Ebbets Field. *National Baseball Hall of Fame*

Right: The Dodgers played their last game at Ebbets Field on September 24, 1957, before moving to the west coast.

SAN DIEGO PADRES

PETCO PARK

Address:
100 Park Boulevard, San Diego
CA 92173
Capacity: 42,445
Opening day: April 8, 2004. San Diego Padres 4, San Francisco Giants 3 (10 innings)
Cost to construct: $449 million
Architect: HOK Sports
Dimensions (ft):
Left Field—334
Left Center—390
Center Field—396
Right Center—391
Right Field—322
Defining feature: Left field Western Metal Supply Co. Building. When the Padres hit a home run a foghorn is sounded.
World Series: None
All-Star Game: 2006, 2016
Memorable moments:
2004 March 11—first game at the park saw the San Diego State Aztecs defeat Houston.
2004 April 15—Mark Loretta hits the Padres' first home run at the stadium.
2005 November 11—The Rolling Stones play a concert at the stadium. Madonna performs there in 2008.
2006 March 18 and 20—the semi-finals and finals of the first World Baseball Classic are played at PETCO. Japan wins the inaugural tournament.
2007 August 4—Barry Bonds hits his 755th homer, tying with Hank Aaron
2008 April 17—Padres and Rockies play a 22-innings game, which the Rockies win 2–1.
2010 May 31—the Padres beat the Mets 18–6.
2010 June 14—Earthquake stops play briefly in the 8th.
2011 April 8—Rain stops play three times and the game against the Dodgers is finished the next day.

Baseball was played in downtown San Diego before there really was a downtown. More than a 130 years later, the bustling city center is home to a much-admired downtown stadium, just blocks from the spot of the first sandlot games.

Petco Park is a "retro" stadium with a distinctly Southern California look. Surrounded by jacaranda trees, water walls, natural stone, and a stucco exterior, the park offers panoramic views of downtown skyscrapers, Mission Bay, Balboa Park, and the arid mountains that surround the city.

Its trademark feature is a left-field warehouse, the turn-of-the-century Western Metal Supply Co. building. Though far smaller than Camden Yard's B&O warehouse, it directly abuts the field, creating an irresistible target for right handed hitters. The left corner of the building holds the left-field foul pole, and each of its four floors contains outdoors seating and a unique perspective on the game.

Unlike the Padres' old home at Qualcomm Stadium, also known as Jack Murphy Field, Petco Park was built exclusively for baseball. The park is intimate, with 20,000 fewer seats than Qualcomm, three decks rather than four, seats located much closer to the field, and all angled toward the pitchers mound. The park boasts a capacity of 46,000, though there are only 42,000 seats, reflecting a range of standing room options for fans who can see the ballgame from the concourse and a variety of porches and terraces, in addition to the center field "Park at the Park," a grass park and picnic area for about 2,500 fans.

The unusual (and much ridiculed) name comes from the San Diego-based retailer of pet supplies, which bought the naming rights reportedly for $60 million over 22 years. Outside, where the early sandlot games were played, the ballpark is anchor to a larger downtown redevelopment project, with plans for a new library, museum, and apartments. Immediately outside the stadium are two noteworthy features. First there is the Palm Court Plaza, the main entrance from the Gaslamp District. This consists of a grid-like pattern of bricks, each placed in a quadrant named after a baseball term and bearing a message from fans. There is also the Park in the Park, an area directly behind the center field area. This contains a Little League infield, Picnic Hill, and a statue of the legendary Tony Gwynn surrounded by 2,000 bricks, again inscribed with fans' messages.

The pitcher-friendly confines of Petco were altered after the 2012 season. The center field walls were moved in (left from 402 to 390 feet, right from 402 feet to 391 feet), and the right field wall from 360 to 349 feet. (It was also lowered to 8 feet.) On top of this, the visiting team bullpen was moved from foul territory in right field to behind the Padres' bullpen. The changes didn't make the ballpark qualify as neutral, but improved batting chances at a franchise that has ranked last in the Major Leagues in runs scored at home four times since opening (2006–2009) and 29th on two occasions (2005, 2011).

There were 101 homers in 2014 but boy! Did all that change in 2015. "Something definitely is up at Petco Park in 2015," said *The San Diego Union-Tribune*, as the number of home runs reached 166, "Whether it's because the Padres struggled on the mound, or packed more punch in their lineup or the new scoreboard blocked the wind … " The fans don't care why!

The Padres' home park added six new dining establishments with local ties to its 2017 food lineup, as well as a nursing station for mothers with new babies. The Breitbard Hall of Fall, a prestigious San Diego sports hall, was moved into the Western Metal Supply Co. building at Petco Park in 2017. The building, which opened in 1909, is embedded in left field with the foul pole a yellow stripe painted on the brick corner. Some 153 athletes' plaques were scheduled to be hung in a concourse inside the Supply building.

Right: The San Diego Padres play against the New York Mets at Petco Park on April 30, 2004.
© David Madison/NewSport/Corbis

Left: The exterior of Petco Park, March 13, 2013, looking toward the Home Plate Gate.
Bernard Gagnon via WikiCommons (CC BY-SA 3.0)

Right: Petco is an attractive, intimate ballpark with breathtaking views over San Diego.
abrowncoat via WikiCommons (CC BY-SA 2.0)

Above: Panorama from left field of Petco Park in San Diego,
California. 12 April 2009
SD Dirk via WikiCommons (CC BY 2.0)

Above and Below Right: Scoreboard details showing the difference between old (Below) on December 20, 2006, and new (Above) on April 18, 2015. Baseball's third-largest video board, all 7,564-square-feet of it coupled with the construction of the 16-story Sempra Energy building may have home run hitting at the ballpark. Something has, because there are a lot more of them than there used to be. Note the Western Metal Supply Co building to the left in both photos.
Jscarreiro via WikiCommons; Val Gonzaga/Bonitavistacrusader

QUALCOMM STADIUM (1969–2003)
Home of the San Diego Padres

The Padres originated in San Diego in 1969, thanks to the considerable efforts of Jack Murphy, sports editor of the San Diego Union, who campaigned for an expansion team to partner the NFL's Chargers. The public voted yes at a referendum and work began on what became the San Diego Stadium—a 166-acre site in Mission Valley. The first MLB game there was on April 8, 1969, and in 1980 the stadium was renamed in honor of Jack Murphy. In 1997 it became Qualcomm Stadium after that company paid $18 million for naming rights. The money was used to fully enclose the ballpark. This helped keep the Padres there until 2003 (their lease had been due to run out at the end of the 1999 season) but they moved to the baseball-only Paetco Park in 2004 leaving the Chargers at Qualcomm.

The Padres took the division title and NL pennant in 1984 but lost the World Series to the Tigers. They had little success otherwise but they attracted increasing crowds particularly from 1996 when they won the division and 1998 when they reached the World Series (although losing again). Seating capacity was much greater at this venue than Petco—reaching 67,544 in 1997 and the best annual figures for the Padres were around 2.5 million.

Opposite: Night view of Qualcomm from above first base. 2003 was the final season for the Padres in Qualcomm Stadium. Constructed in 1967, "the Q" had been the Padres' home since their inaugural season in 1969. It hosted a pair of World Series (1984 and 1998) and a pair of Major League Baseball All-Star games (1978 and 1992).
Digitalballparks.com

Above Left: Qualcomm's capacity was 67,544 in 1997.
Digitalballparks.com

Left: The then recently completed San Diego Stadium, which could seat 50,000 and was convertible between football to baseball configurations, seen on April 4, 1967.
Getty Images

Far Left: Opening day national anthem before the April 1, 1997, game between the New York Mets and San Diego. The Padres won the game 12–5.
Jed Jacobsohn/Allsport via Getty Images

SAN FRANCISCO GIANTS

AT&T PARK

Aka: Pac Bell Park (2000–03), SBC Park (2003–05)
Address:
801 Third Street
San Francisco, CA 94107
Capacity: 41,915
Opening day: April 11, 2000—Los Angeles Dodgers 6, San Francisco Giants 5
Cost to construct: $319 million
Architect: HOK Sports
Dimensions (ft):
Left Field—339
Left Center—364
Center Field—399
Right Center—421
Right Field—309
Defining feature: McCovey Cove
Most expensive seat: $75
Cheapest seat: $10
World Series: 2002, 2010, 2012, 2014
All-Star Game: 2007
Memorable Moments:
2000 May 1—Barry Bonds hits the first regulation game ball into McCovey Cove, off Mets' Rich Rodriguez.
2002 August 9—Bonds joins Hank Aaron, Babe Ruth, and Willie Mays as the only players to hit 600 HRs.
2002 October 14—Kenny Lofton hits a two-out, ninth-inning single to beat the St. Louis Cardinals 2–1 and send the Giants to their first World Series since 1962: they lose to the Angels.
2010 October 28—Nate Schierholtz's catch wins game 2 against the Rangers 9–0. Three days later the Giants win their first World Series since 1954.
2012 October 25—A shutout win in game 2 of the World Series gives the Giants a 2–0 lead over the Tigers. Two more wins in Detroit and the title returns.
2014 October 26—Game 5 of the World Series sees Madison Bumgarner shut out the Royals and the Giants head for Kansas up 3–2. They win in the 7th game and Bumgarner is World Series MVP.

Ask any five-year old. There is a primal satisfaction that comes from splashing a solid object into a body of water.

The Giants have taken this proposition to major-league heights at AT&T Park, where the chilly waters of the San Francisco Bay sit a tantalizing 352 feet from home plate.

There is much that is appealing about the Giants' new home. The park is small and its dimensions intimate. The sight lines are engineered exclusively for baseball. The field is asymmetrical with a 25-foot high brick wall just 309 feet from home plate, the closest foul pole in the majors. The view beyond the outfield is as beautiful an urban landscape as can be imagined.

But for all its charms, nothing compares to the childishly irresistible anticipation that a powerful left handed hitter might clear the 25-foot brick wall in right field, and plop a home run into the water named after the Giants' Hall of Fame first baseman Willie McCovey. The Giants have such a hitter, and SBC is unmistakably the park that (Barry) Bonds built. Just as the Yankees erected a short right-field fence in 1923 for their star left hander, Babe Ruth, the Giants built the ballpark for Bonds, the marquee power hitter of his time. As the 2004 season opened, only seven other players had "gone Bay," but Bonds himself had done it 27 times, thrilling capacity crowds who were just warming up after four decades at frigid Candlestick Park.

In the end Bonds did it 35 times between 2000 and 2007. At the time of writing in spring 2016, the total had risen to 105.

Just as fans gather on Chicago's Waveland Avenue for the chance at a home run ball, sailors, kayakers, and other boaters fill McCovey Cove during Giants games, their eyes fixed on the right field fence. The location is so close that when the Yankees Jorge Posada hit the ball into the cove during an exhibition game, the ball was scooped up by boater Mike Quinby, who promptly threw it back onto the field on a fly.

AT&T Park was built in the mold of Camden Yards. Rather than the B&O warehouse in right field, it is the Bay, with stunning vistas of the East Bay hills and the Bay Bridge from the upper deck. Architects resisted even more sweeping views in order to reduce the wind, and to give Bonds a better shot at reaching the Bay. Temperatures are not nearly as cold as at windy Candlestick, where former Giants pitcher Stu Miller was famously blown off the mound during the 1961 All-Star Game. Still, you won't catch many locals wearing short sleeves at night.

The inside is bustling with activity, from an 80-foot long Coca Cola bottle in left field, which houses slides for kids, and a 27-foot baseball glove at its spout, to a miniature SBC park, where kids can smack Wiffle balls over the fence. Outside, a statue of Willie Mays is a central meeting spot near the park's main entrance, and another of McCovey overlooks his cove on the Bay side.

Known as Pac Bell Park when it opened, the name changed in 2004 after Texas-based communications company SBC (Southwest Bell Corp.) bought the local phone company, putting some San Franciscans in the awkward position of clamoring for the park's original corporate name. SBC is the first privately financed park in Major League Baseball since Dodger Stadium in 1962.

When SBC merged with AT&T Corp. in 2005 the park's name changed again.

There have been many upgrades since the park opened: the wifi technology has been improved constantly and was particularly in demand during the 2014 World Series. The various suites have been upgraded and new Dugout Stores constructed. In 2015 A new center-field LED videoboard replaced the former AT&T Tri-Vision display directly beneath the Mitsubishi DiamondVision scoreboard, and the clubhouse was renovated. The Giants and AT&T began the 2017 season with the longest sellout streak in the National League at 489 games. Including 25 more playoff games to make the total 514, this gave the Giants the longest such streak in Major League Baseball. Also, having 31,000 season-ticket holders was the greatest number in team history.

On the concessions front, the Giants introduced a 100 percent organic menu.

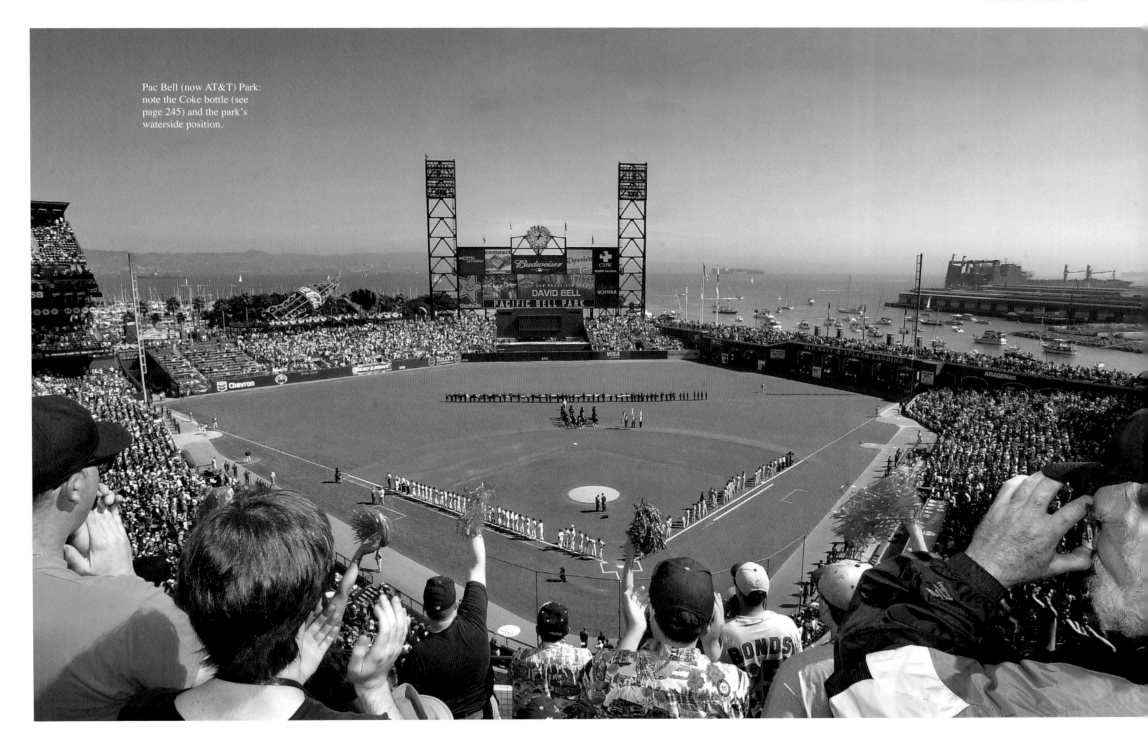

Pac Bell (now AT&T) Park:
note the Coke bottle (see
page 245) and the park's
waterside position.

Right: Aerial View of SBC Park.
Douglas Peebles/Corbis

Above and Below: AT&T Park on August 1, 2006. Note McCovey Cove (at right in above photo), a splash target for left-handed sluggers throughout the league. The Cove is separated from the right field seats by a promenade, popular with casual fans interested in catching a play or two while passing by on a summer's walk. It happened 13 times in 2014—eight of those by visitors including Carlos González for the third time, and five by Giants including Brandon Belt for the fourth time.
Daniel Schwen via WikiCommons (CC BY-SA 2.5)

Right: General view of SBC Park during the national anthem before game 3 of the National League Championship series between the Cardinals and the Giants on October 12, 2002. The Giants lost but went on to win the series 4–1.
Matthew Stockman/Getty Images

Left: Stand-in Pitcher Kirk Rueter—#46 of the San Francisco Giants—throws a pitch during game five of the National League Championship series against the Cardinals on October 14, 2002. The Giants won the game 2–1 and the series 4–1. Behind him are left field bleachers and, above them, the Coca-Cola Fan Lot and Giant 1927 Old-Time Four-Fingered Baseball Glove. The Coke bottle is 80-foot long, contains viewing platforms and four slides, two 56-foot-long curving slides (the "Guzzler") and two 20-foot-long twisting slides (the "Twist-Off"). The baseball mitt is 26-foot-high, 32-foot-wide and 12-foot-deepand made of steel and fiberglass.
Getty Images

Far Left: Fans stand in a moment of silence in a pre-game ceremony in honor of the victims of September 11 before the game between the Dodgers and the Giants at Pacific Bell Park on September 11, 2002.
Getty Images

Right: In recognition of the Hall of Fame player who wore the Giants' number 24 for 22 seasons, this nine-foot bronze statue of the great Willie Mays welcomes fans to the entrance to the newly renamed SBC Park at 24 Willie Mays Plaza. The 24 palm trees that line the plaza are another part of the tribute to one of baseball's most honored and beloved players.
Scott Sommerdorf/San Francisco Chronicle

Inset, Right: At 5:04 on October 17, 1989, a 7.1 earthquake struck the San Francisco Bay Area as the Giants and Oakland A's were preparing for game three of that year's World Series. This photo shows the scene at Candlestick Park moments after the quake hit, rattling the press boxes, knocking out power, and prompting a giant roar from the shaken fans. The game was postponed minutes later. The A's went on to sweep the Giants in four games.
John O'Hara/San Francisco Chronicle

CANDLESTICK PARK
(1960–1999)
Home of the San Francisco Giants

The New York Giants moved to the west coast the same year the Dodgers moved to LA—1957. Both teams started playing in the National League's West Division since 1969. The Giants started at Seals Stadium before moving to the Candlestick Park, on San Francisco Bay. It was lovely when it was warm but often cold, windy, and above all, foggy. Ito make matters wore, the baseball-only facility was expanded to cater for the arrival of NFL's San Francisco 49ers and the stadium was enclosed. All that did was make the swirling wind even less predictable.

The Giants have had some good years in the Stick, winning the West Division title on three occasions (1971, 1989, and 1997), and appeared in two World Series: They went down to the New York Yankees 4–3 in 1962 and were swept by their cross-bay rivals in Oakland in a famous series that was disrupted when the Bay Area was hit by an earthquake a few minutes before Game 3.

Left: September 30, 1999: A general view of the last game at 3 Com Park, commonly known as Candlestick Park, between the Dodgers and the Giants. The Dodgers defeated the Giants 9–4.
Jed Jacobsohn/Allsport via Getty Images

Left: Exterior view of Candlestick park as boats bring fans in for opening day game against St. Louis Casrdinals, April 12, 1960.
Jon Brenneis/Time Life Pictures/Getty Images

Far Left: General view of Candlestick Park, home of the San Francisco Giants in 1989.
Otto Greule Jr/Getty Images

Left: Candlestick Park as built, with scoreboard above the batter's eye in center-field.
National Baseball Hall of Fame

Far Left: Candlestick Park, was enclosed in 1971–1972 to allow the NFL San Francisco 49ers to play there. Other changes included a video scoreboard in left field and Astroturf (accounting for the markings seen in this photograph), which would be replaced by grass in 1979.
National Baseball Hall of Fame

251

Left: Candlestick Park, 1999.
Joseph Sohm; Visions of America/Corbis

This Page: Between 1883 and 1957 today's San Francisco Giants were based in New York, originally named the Gothams and then the Giants. While there they played their home games most of the time at the Polo Grounds, where they won five of the franchise's eight World Series wins and 17 of its 24 NL pennants. As can be seen from these views of the Polo Grounds, it was an idiosyncratic ballpark, with a distinctive footprint and dimensions of:

Left Field: 279ft
Left-Center: 450ft
Center Field: 483ft
Right-Center: 449ft
Right Field: 258ft

Hitters loved it because of its short measurements down the foul lines, with the overhanging left field upper deck especially susceptible to home runs. *National Baseball Hall of Fame*

This Page: Interior views of the Polo Grounds.
Associated Press/ National Baseball Hall of Fame; Corbis/ National Baseball Hall of Fame

Following Page: An aerial view of AT&T Park, then known as Pacific Bell Park, framed by the San Francisco skyline as fans arrive about an hour before the first pitch the park's first game ever, an exhibition between the Giants and the Milwaukee Brewers in March of 2000.
Brant Ward/San Francisco Chronicle

INDEX